In Formation

How to Gain the 71% Advantage

Larry W. Dennis, Sr.

Rising Tide Publishing
Portland, Oregon

In Formation

First Printing 1997
Second Printing 2002

Rising Tide Publishing
36280 N.E. Wilsonville Rd.
Newberg, OR 97132
Email: turbo@turbomgmt.com

ISBN 0-89716-674-4
Library of Congress No. 96-071486

Cover Design: Richard Ferguson
Editor: Christy Scattarella
Layout Design: Malia A. Johnson

Manufactured in the U.S.A.

Other books by Larry W. Dennis, Sr.
Empowering Leadership
How to Turbo Charge You
Repeat Business
Making Moments Matter
The Great Baseball Cap

Dedication

---

*This book is dedicated to the
men and women in organizations,
both large and small, who struggle through the
pain of change required to make the most
effective use of all resources.*

They enrich our world in three important ways:

First, by creating empowered team members;

*Second, by providing greater value from the
resources with which they are entrusted;*

*Third, by being an example for the world to
model, creating a richer place for us all.*

Foreword

Larry W. Dennis, Sr., has done what is rarely done in a management book. Larry has written a book which is based on sound psychological principle and provides excellent leadership instruction that is easy to follow; it is practical! Anyone reading this book- management at any level - will find very practical advice and guidelines combined with sound management principles. The precepts are "workable." Mr. Dennis has 24 years' experience in working on the front line managers at all levels, in all areas of leadership - he is not just a theorist. If you are genuinely *In Formation* you will experience the "71% Advantage." I recommend *In Formation* MOST highly!

Dr. Jack H. Holland, PHD, MBA
Stanford Emeritus Professor of Management

Table Of Contents

1 Words That Work 3
   What Is Communication? 4
   Cool Hand Luke 7
   Smooth Sailing 8
   WIIFM 10
   Specificity Empowers Your Words 11
   Choosing Words 12
   Admit Vulnerability 15
   Empower With Animation And Enthusiasm 16

2 Vision For The Voyage 19
   Why Look Beyond? 20
   Creating a Vision Statement 24
   Mission: The Purpose Behind The Vision 28

3 Values For The Voyage 35
   The Value of Consistency 35
   I Quit 36
   The Ethical Dilemma 37
   Committing Values To Heart 39
   Justice 44
   The Basics 45
   Values In Formation 48

4   Champion Change 53
     Cultural Change 54
     DS x MV x FS > RC 55
     A Change For The Better 58
     Quality Steering Team 60
     Effects Of Change 61
     Mastering The Forces Of Change 63

5   Longing For Belonging 69
     Three Basics Of A Performance Team 71
     Moving Toward Team Spirit 72
     Functions Of A Performance Team 74
     Benefits Of Performance Teams: 76
     Stages Of Performance Team Development: 78
     Forming, Storming, Norming, Performing 78
     Forming 78
     Storming 79
     Norming 80
     Performing 81

6   Customer Commitment 85
     Shirt Off Your Back 85
     Identifying The Customer 87
     Listen To Your Customer 90
     Lasting Impressions 92

7   Productive Processes 99
     Study The Process 100
     Proper Process Empowers 103
     Steps To Improve Your Process 105
     EEEEEE 110
     Process Development Comes In Many Colors ... 111

8 Meaningful Measures 115
      Learning Organization 117
      Measurement 118
      System Performance 120
      Benchmarking 121
      Performance Criteria Data 123
      Feedback 124
      Measuring and Chartering Suppliers 126
      Measure For Measure 128

9 Determining The Destination 133
      Setting Goals 135
      Kaizen 139

10 Tactical Training 143
      Midnight Oil 145
      Around The Corner 147
      Train To Fit 150
      Who Should Do The Training? 154

11 Keeping Commitments 157
      Salvaged Opportunity 159
      Cleaned Up 161
      Who Will Do What By When? 163
      Aligning Agreements 165
      Don't Open With Excuses 168

12 Embracing Encouragement 171
      Encourage Mints 171
      Provide Courage Through Encouragement 173
      Charged Up 175
      Merry Christmas 176
      Sweatshirts 178

Accepting Praise 179
Mailing The Mailman 180

13 Caring Coaching 187
Remodel 189
Secrets of Caring Coaching 190
The Extra Mile 191
A Pinch In Time 193
Pulling Teeth 194
'But' Method 195
#@&*! 197
Sub-Contractors 199
Review 200
Wandering Around 202

14 Courageous Correction 207
Fault Finding 207
Candy Bar 209
Two Ways To Correct 210
Bid Day 212
Moving Into Alignment 214
Take-Off's 215
Off Course 217
Start With Praise 218
Pain In The Butt 219
Discharging 221

15 Practical Problem Solving 225
Fogged In 225
A Philosophy of Problem Solving 227
When Does A Problem Exist? 228
All Washed Up 229
Problem Solving Wheel 232

Tips On Defining The Problem 232
Diagrams For Problem-Solving 233
Getting Help 235

16 Meaningful Meetings 239
Stumbling Blocks 240
Planning The Environment 243
Planning Effective Meetings 244
Team Meeting Preparation Checklist: 247
Brainstorm Success 248
Starting Your Meeting 249
Develop a Code of Conduct 253
Meetings Matter 254
Speaking Before Groups 255

17 Listening Leader 263
Go Fish 263
Slip Sliding Away 265
Make Time To Listen 268
Focus Groups 269
Mom 270
Listen With Empathy 271
Listen to Lead 273
Active vs. Passive Listening 275

18 Loyal Leadership 281
Jump In 281
Going The Distance 283
If You Blow It, Show It 285
Empowering Leaders Manage Emotions 287
Empowering Leaders Serve 292
"And A Little Child Shall Lead Them" 294
It's An Old Story 296

Introduction

It was a cool, quiet Sunday morning. My wife, Donna Lee, and I were driving along in the country. Suddenly, a joyful honking from above broke the silence. We looked out the sunroof to see a flock of geese, perhaps a hundred, soaring gracefully above us. I watched as the geese glided across the sky in a near perfect 'V' formation and listened to their loud, continuous honking. As the formation started to break up, the lead goose dropped back in the formation while another took its place. They organized and reorganized their formation, struggling, it seemed, to re-form into that near perfect 'V'.

Why is the 'V' formation so important to the geese? Scientists have learned that as each bird flaps its wings, it creates an uplift for the bird immediately following. With no additional effort, the whole flock increases flying range by at least 71 percent when flying in a 'V' formation. We have discovered that leaders of successful organizations benefit by following the example of the deceptively simple goose. People who share a common vision, direction and sense of community reach their goals more quickly and easily because they travel on the uplifting thrust of one another.

Whenever a goose falls out of formation, it suddenly feels the drag and resistance of flying solo. It quickly moves back into the 'V' formation to take advantage of the lifting power from the birds immediately in front. We demonstrate that we gain the same advantages as geese when we stay aligned and *in formation* with those headed in our same direction.

When the lead goose tires, it rotates to the back of the formation and another goose flies to the point position. It pays to take turns doing hard tasks and sharing leadership with others. High performance organizations create a climate in which people fly to point positions in their respective areas of influence. Dynamic organizations, like geese, are not static. They continuously reorder themselves to achieve peak performance.

Geese are constantly honking from behind to encourage those up front to maintain their speed. They are always in communication. High performance organizations continuously 'honk' support through words of appreciation, recognizing that encouragement motivates the team to peak performance.

Even at times when a goose falls ill, a pair of fellow geese may fall out of formation and follow it down to the ground to offer help and protection. They remain with the injured goose until it can fly again, and then they launch out together, eventually catching up with their formation. People who are part of an *in formation* organization stand by one another in every department, every specialty, every level of the organization. When a team member flounders, the team willingly assists rather than watching complacently as the team member struggles to recover.

Would you like to enhance your team's performance by 71 percent? *In Formation* will equip you and your team with the same advantages geese enjoy! By following the simple guidelines and principles outlined in this book, your organization will fly farther, faster, with no additional effort, keeping your organization out in front.

Since 1966, I have worked with the management teams of thousands of organizations to help them improve the sharing of information so they could fly *in formation* and gain the 71 percent advantage. My company, Turbo Management Systems, has helped bring organizations into formation and empower their teams to world-class performance. Some of our well known clients have included Nabisco Brands, Midas Mufflers, Fox Affiliate, Ryerson Steel, Hewlett Packard, GenTel and IBM.

Turbo Management Systems is a management, development and training company that designs and delivers programs to create a team culture. These programs enhance quality, customer satisfaction, and ultimately, result in profits that exceed expectations. Turbo's Leadership Development, Management Advance and Performance Team LABs have helped our clients empower their teams to peak performance. Throughout *In formation*, you will hear from clients who participated in these LABs, where they have honed their leadership skills. Their organizations, in turn, have evolved into self-directing, problem-solving performance teams that are soaring to new levels of accomplishment.

Now, you too can benefit from these same strategies, processes and insights to ensure continuous improvement. You will learn the difference between 'pseudo' teams and 'true performance' teams. You will create an organization where all team members experience fulfillment as they strive towards increasing company profitability. By following the techniques outlined throughout *In formation*, you will lead your organization into a more confident future.

The Example

I tried to tell you.
You didn't hear a word I said.
I begged and pleaded.
You didn't turn your head.
I cajoled and threatened.
You stiffened and fled.

I argued, stomped my feet,
Piled up statistics ten feet deep.
I searched to find something I could say or do
To get through to you.

Finally, I told you a story and gave you an example.
Your response was, "Why all the excitement?
The example is ample."

One simple personal example?
Is that all it took?
Is that all I had to say?
Now you're ready to see it my way?

I can hear you say,
"Examples? They're so hard to find,
So difficult to keep in mind!"

I guess I could agree.
Examples may be hard to see,
Especially when your mind is on you —
You're always in a stew,
Running here, running there,
Never able to be aware

I've decided to become aware —
If necessary to even stare,
Yes, to care, prepare to share.

I tell a simple story,
One from my life,
Not much glory.
I play it down, but still I'm specific
And give details. They sound terrific.

I tell my listeners what I've learned
I let them decide for themselves
If I've earned the right to advise
They assure me I'm quite wise.
And would you believe it?

The simple, fun way to achieve it
Is to give an example
From our own personal lives!

-Larry W. Dennis, Sr.

>>> 1

Words That Work

"Speech is the power to persuade, to convert, to compel.
Persuasion is condensing some daily experience
into a glowing symbol."

Ralph Waldo Emerson

The year was 1948. Joe was pumping gas at his dad's filling station in the tiny town of McMinnville, Oregon. Every few days, a fellow in a 1938 Buick, one of the regulars, would pull in and buy $2 worth of gasoline. Of course, back then that could get you almost 20 gallons. One day the old Buick pulled up steaming and boiling over.

"I popped the hood and looked inside. I saw some bubbling going on around where the head bolted to the block and immediately I knew it must be a blown head-gasket. I pulled the dip stick and found water on it," Joe said.

The customer hollered out, "I think I've got a radiator problem."

Joe yelled back over the racket, "I think it's in your head."

The customer jumped out of his car and stormed into the gas station. Joe looked inside and could see a heated discussion between his father and the customer. The customer stormed back out, got in his car, drove away and did not return for over a month. One night when he finally came back in, he sheepishly got out of his car and apologized to Joe for having raced off in such a huff. "You were right. The problem was in the cylinder head!" he said.

Joe, who today heads the international marketing division for a dental equipment manufacturer, said he learned a valuable lesson back in 1948. Communication is everything. Here we are, virtually half a century later, blessed with high-technology interaction unimaginable in those days. Still, many leaders continue to stumble over that fundamental message: *Communication, the effective transference of information, is everything.*

What Is Communication?

Communication is the transference of thoughts, feelings and ideas leading to understanding. We communicate through words, tones, mannerisms, gestures and, sometimes, silence. A meaningful connection occurs when the receiver experiences, understands and knows what you, the sender, experience, understand and know. Through effective communication, we gain the *information* that enables us to stay *in formation*. The single most important ability of the empowering leader is the ability to communicate effectively. The leader is responsible for ensuring that *information* flows in a manner that creates the formation for maximum success.

The word "communication" comes from the same source as "community" and "communion" and means relationship. At its deepest level, communication means real understanding. When you break the word understanding down you get UNDER-STANDING, the foundation upon which we stand. We fail to recognize that the real problem is more often a lack of understanding than lack of *information.* Without understanding, no matter how many facts we pour into people's minds, full communication will not occur.

Understanding goes back to the colloquial expression to "take a stand" or "stand up for." At the heart of real communication is the desire to be understood. Poor relationships stem from misunderstanding. It is the responsibility of the sender, the initiator of the communication, to be understood, not the responsibility of the receiver to understand. Whenever we say, "They did not understand," we have forgotten one fundamental of communication: committing yourself to getting the message across.

Unless we effectively communicate our interest, determination and attempts to lead, subsequent attempts will be fruitless. Everything we do as a leader revolves around the rapport we establish with others. Empowering leaders have learned that great communication is like a ray of sunlight. The more concentrated your communication, the greater its intensity. Often, the more sparing we are with words, the more penetrating our message.

It is important to recognize that our communication style results more from habit than thought. Developing new skills requires commitment and determination. We will only become proficient communicators by replacing old patterns with a new, more dynamic style of speech. As we sharpen our skills, we exercise responsibility as empowering leaders to get our point across more effectively.

This book will help you acquire the communication skills needed to provide your team with the *information* required to get *in formation* so you can fulfill your organization's mission and realize its vision. When every member of the team is in alignment, we achieve synergism. The whole truly is greater than the sum of its parts, allowing us to far exceed collectively what any of us can do individually. Sometimes it seems departments are pulling at right angles, if not in opposite directions. When teams become aligned, they achieve the 71 percent performance advantage.

How does an organization create this kind of synergistic teamwork? Effective communication is the key. During our training sessions with organizations, we have found poor communication or a lack of information to be the most frequent complaint of team members. Field crews do not know what is going on in the office, scheduling is not in harmony with purchasing or manufacturing, and sales seem to pull in the opposite direction of manufacturing and marketing.

In 1989, while waiting at the hospital for the birth of my granddaughter, I heard a "Wa-a-a-a-a" echoing down the hall. I said, "I bet that's her!" I ran over to the viewing window where I saw my son, Larry Jr., proudly holding up Alexandra Michelle Dennis for me to see. My first experience with our granddaughter was hearing her "Wa-a-a-a-a". We all communicate from our first "Wa-a-a-a-a" to our last sigh, and we communicate everywhere in between. The problem I had with Alexandra Michelle is that when she cried, I was not sure what she wanted.

Sometimes, when we make noises, the people around us may not be sure what we want. By practicing the principles and guidelines in this book, you will be in a far better position to transfer information effectively. You will utilize the skills central to empowering leadership and building a high performance team.

I remember hearing noises of uncertainty from the top management of a large retailer. This uncertainty resulted in inefficiencies and lost profits and sales. We worked with the ten top executives, the board chair and the senior vice presidents. The average tenure of these key executives was over seventeen years. Most of them grew up together in their careers at the company.

These executives talked as if they had to wait for permission before they could implement new projects. The distribution center manager was waiting for permission to reorganize shifts, provide pay incentives and initiate staff training. The merchandising manager was waiting for permission to narrow and clarify lines of specialty to create a market niche. The MIS manager was waiting for permission to hire the staff necessary to achieve 100% scanability at the cash registers. The operations manager was waiting for permission to institute customer service training. The president was waiting for permission to implement a much needed integrated advertising campaign. The company was out of formation. And everyone interpreted the next person's lack of initiative as incompetence.

As I watched this play out, I said, "Where is your management team? Where are the people who can make the call?" They looked at one another and said, "We are all here." I said, "Now let's make some decisions and move on."

Cool Hand Luke

If you have seen the classic movie "Cool Hand Luke" with Paul Newman, you may remember the scene in the middle of the night in which the inmate Luke is down in the ditch digging. The warden, nicknamed "Captain," has done all he could to beat the Newman character into submission, but he refuses to cave in. As a last desperate measure, Captain tries to illustrate his message by forcing Luke to dig a six-foot-deep ditch. Captain stands over the hole, peers in and says, "What we've got here is a failure to communicate."

We cannot force others to understand us. It is our responsibility to recognize that the persons with whom we communicate bring their own biases, vested interests, points of view, fears and previous experiences to each interaction. These biases and preconceived notions influence how successful we are in transferring information.

Smooth Sailing

During the entire first meeting for a boat dealer, the service manager was negative and disruptive. Later, as we spoke one-on-one, he chewed me out. He said that while he had been in the Army, a consultant came on post who was a "yes-man," a dupe for the Commanding Officer. This manager saw me as the "dupe" for the owner of the marina. When he came to the breakfast meeting, he did not see me, he only saw the "army dupe" for the marina owner. He re-lived his unpleasant army experience. He filtered all I said through an incident that had occurred over a decade earlier. It was my job to understand his viewpoint and find ways to relate to him.

Many times, the mistakes we make in attempts to transfer information stem from our individual differences in point of view and attitude. We need to understand the other person's point of view so we can position our communication in terms of the other person's interests. When people from Sales and Accounting meet, they bring their own assumptions and viewpoints. When Production and Distribution get together, they bring their preconceived notions and agendas. Plan your communication. What could be blocking your meaningful communication? Understanding the barriers opens the way to a meaningful transference of what we want to communicate. Ask yourself, "What might cause the other person to fail to embrace, listen to, and understand my message, my idea or my thoughts?"

If our attitudes coincide, then successful communication will be a snap. If there is a 50/50 chance of being misunderstood, you will be misunderstood. Remember: The person who is only 20% informed, which is all too typical, usually has a negative attitude.

When Turbo Management Systems conducted its Employee Opinion Survey at a steel distribution warehouse, it became immediately clear there was a morale problem. Several people wrote in the comment section of the survey: "Are we going to be in business next year?" "I hope we are still in business a year from now". "We need to do something if we are going to stay in business".

We ultimately discovered the persons who were picking and loading the orders and driving the trucks were concerned about their jobs because they were no longer seeing the names of old familiar customers. They had been pulling, loading and delivering high carbon steel to those customers for years and suddenly, those customers vanished. This led to the conclusion that the business was diminishing, sales declining, and maybe, those loaders and drivers would lose their jobs. When we're provided only partial information, we jump to conclusions, and they are often negative.

As it turns out, the elimination of those customers was a strategy the branch manager had developed. The organization planned to eliminate low margin, high carbon steel from its product lines and replace it with high alloy steel, which is easier to move and store and has higher margins. Unfortunately, the people on the floor had not been informed of this strategy. Although there were many new customers, what riveted the workers' attention was the elimination of old familiar customers. They perceived that the company was failing. Management's point of view was that the new marketing strategy must be kept secret. Managers feared word would get out to existing customers of the old high carbon steel before the warehouse was emptied of existing inventory.

If you want to have high morale, an open flow of *information* is a must. Keep everyone in the loop.

WIIFM

To foster a spirit of cooperation, recognize that everyone is listening to the same station: WIIFM — "What's In It For Me?" Answer the WIIFM question early in all your communications designed to influence others. Quite simply, tell them how they will benefit. Do not tell them what you need and want, and do not make demands. Instead, tell them how they will benefit, prosper, progress and feel better. Otherwise, why should anyone listen to your ideas? It is not enough to just throw ideas out and expect people to run with them. We cannot expect our team to embrace our every little thought. We must package, arrange and mold our ideas into an appealing, irresistible presentation. Answer the WIIFM question in every presentation you make.

Specificity Empowers Your Words

Generalities mean little to our listeners. If you are vague, your message will not penetrate the minds of your team members and they will forget what you've said. Your message loses impact. Good communicators ask themselves, "Why be general when I can be specific?" Why say "car" when you can say "a blue 1996 Cadillac Seville"? Why say "young child" when you can say "10-year-old Barry" or "16-year-old Mary"? Why say "morning" when you can say "7:05 a.m."? We tend to generalize due to our own lack of awareness and just plain mental laziness. Chaotic thoughts are given order by words. Look for and find the specific words that will make the greatest possible impact on your listener.

Kim, a project manager for a general contractor, told one of our Leadership Development LABs about his fly fishing trip. His specifically detailed description really made the trip come alive for me: "We were fly fishing for huge tarpons, which were swimming all around our 22-foot fiberglass skiff. Mike and I were watching Gary and Andy in the other skiff as they frantically cast their huge 3/0 tarpon flies with their heavy 12 weight fly rods toward several pods of 100 pound tarpons. Andy, standing 6'3" and weighing 240 pounds, was in the middle of the skiff casting toward a pod of tarpons that were just descending into murky green waters. I watched as he rapidly made a back cast with his 550 grain shooting head and then powerfully double-hauled his forward cast toward his oncoming quarry. As Andy's huge fly streaked forward, its razor-sharp, stainless-steel point found the guide's nose. The hook penetrated completely through it as the force of the collision jolted his head violently to the right. I cringed as the guide calmly removed the fly from his bleeding nose and told Andy 'no problemo'."

Choosing Words

*"Words are living things. You put them down, and
they wiggle around. You cut them, and they bleed."*
                                        Ralph Waldo Emerson

I facilitated a problem-solving meeting for one of our
clients. During our meeting, the direct supervisor of the group
participated more than was appropriate. He kept saying, "You
guys...you guys..." Later, he asked me for feedback. I asked
him what he felt he could have done differently. He was as-
tute enough to understand that he should have talked less and
listened more. Still, he missed the fact that he was using a
phrase that separated him from the team, especially the fe-
male members.

Every word matters. In the case of some pivotal words,
the slightest change in a word can make a major difference in
the impact, import and significance of the message. Think
before you speak. When you have chosen your words wisely
for maximum impact, you will achieve the results you want
easier and faster. Others will respond to you and give you
their full cooperation.

Here are some great examples of words with different meanings than the sender intended:

Donna Lee, my wife, has been a hospice volunteer
for almost a decade. She returned from a monthly training
session once and told me about one of the volunteer's experiences. The volunteer had gone to the hospital to visit with her
patient. While she sat by the bedside holding the frail little
old woman's hand, the patient said, "I'll be going home next
week." In hospice language that means, "I'm going home to
die." The volunteer responded with a warm voice saying,
"How do you feel about that?" The patient said, "I have aides."

The volunteer's heart leaped up into her throat. She thought to herself, "This poor dear woman has AIDS." She tried not to register her pain and asked the same question over again, "How do you feel about that?" The little lady's response was, "Oh, it's wonderful. One aide will be visiting in the morning and the other aide will be coming in the afternoon."

If she had said to the hospice volunteer in the early seventies, "I have aides," the hospice volunteer would have thought that she had nurses or other help coming. A word that used to mean "help" is now one of the most feared words in the English language — a clear example of communication breakdown.

John, a superintendent for an electrical contractor, told our Leadership Development LAB: "In June of 1967, I went back to my home town in Iowa. It was the first time I had taken my wife back to Iowa to meet my family; she's from the West Coast, born and raised. We were invited out to dinner by a couple of friends from my old high school days. One area to note is the terminology of dinner in Iowa is the noon meal, and supper is used to describe the evening meal. We were under the impression that we were going to have a meal with our friends at 6:00 p.m. We were shocked and surprised when we received a call at 2:00 p.m. wondering if we were coming to the noon dinner. Due to our interpretation of dinner, we were two hours late for our reunion meal. Boy, did we have egg on our faces.

The lesson I learned from this experience is the importance of spelling out in exact detail what I mean for all future engagements. I learned to never assume that my listener has the same definition or understanding of terminology. Be specific. When there is any room for doubt, confirm by asking questions and be sure that your listener understands your full meaning. The benefit you will gain is error-free performance. Your customer, internal or external, will receive their deliveries in the form expected on time, every time."

Only a few short years ago, when we heard someone say "fax," they were referring to FACTS — reality, truth. Today, when we hear someone say "fax," they are referring to the electronic transfer of data. Cellular meant the make-up of the human or animal body. Today, it refers to a kind of radio communication. Words that may have special meaning for us may make others less receptive to our message. Look for and find words that make the greatest positive impact on your listener.

Mark Twain said "The difference in a word and the right word is the difference in lightning and a lightning bug," a lesson I learned early on. I spent part of my childhood in the boot-heel of Southeastern Missouri — Poplar Bluff, where summer nights were a treat after the 100-degree days. My two younger brothers and I would catch lightning bugs and put them in a Mason jar to watch them flicker. I still associate the smell of honeysuckle with those summer nights and lightning bugs. When I close my eyes, I can hear the creak of the old porch swing and see the flicker of lightning bugs dancing in the dew-covered honeysuckle. I can still see the brilliant, flashing heat lightning, without rain —a bluish-purple flash in the sky. After a long pause, the loud clap of thunder. One summer night, a lightning bolt struck my grandmother's beloved weeping willow tree. That great giant had shaded over half of the backyard. The lightning sheared it to a quarter of its former stature in a split second. The lightning bugs my brothers and I caught were powerless creatures compared to the strength of lightning, like the bolt that struck my grandmother's willow.

Choose words that have the power of a lightning bolt!

Admit Vulnerability

I watched the partner of one of our client organizations stand in front of the team. With tears streaming down his face he ended a long, heart-felt speech by saying, "I've learned to eliminate dogmatic declarations, and that when I compromise, I'm a winner." He allowed himself to show his vulnerability in front of his organization. When former President Bush made his 50th Anniversary presentation at Pearl Harbor, he broke into tears. Some may say, "Shame on you; men don't cry!" How limiting this kind of thinking can be!

The lesson I learned as I watched these important leaders let down their guard is the power, the authenticity and the credibility in vulnerability.

For authentic communication to exist, you need to be courageous enough to go beyond intellectual conceptualizing. You must invite other persons to empathize with you. Communication is not a cold, logical transfer between two machines; it is influenced and affected by feelings and emotions. If we do not portray our genuine warmth, friendliness, firmness or sincerity, then we shortchange our message. We are not Star Trek's relentlessly logical Spock. We are full of biases, prejudices, judgments and personal agendas.

The action I call you to is to stop being guarded and start letting your real feelings show. Some men keep their guard up because our culture has trained them that showing sensitivity is weak or feminine. Women frequently remain guarded so they won't be perceived as frail or weak. The truth is it takes more strength to show vulnerability than to hide your feelings. Your ego may protest. Still, let the real you shine through. Then watch as your communication illuminates others and your ability to impact grows.

Empower With Animation And Enthusiasm

It is difficult to communicate conviction, commitment and determination without the appropriate accompanying animation and enthusiasm. As my son, Larry Jr., and I were leaving a service club luncheon, Larry Jr. turned to me and said of the luncheon speaker, "That man will never wear out."

I asked, "What do you mean?"

My son replied, "He has no moving parts."

Are you using an appropriate amount of animation? Do you feel enthusiastic about your message? Are you infusing others with your enthusiasm? We all have seen people who are too animated, whose animation does not reinforce their point, and others who move like mechanical robots. Remember, your manner of speaking is just as important as the subject matter. Language is merely the instrument of your ideas — truth and conviction are its source. William Blake said, "The eyes are the windows to the soul." Looking away signals lack of self-confidence or a lack of conviction. We have heard people say, "Can you look me straight in the eye and say that?" The person who does not make good eye contact lacks credibility. Think about your body language. Crossing your arms could indicate defensiveness. Stuffing your hands in your pockets could indicate an overly casual, relaxed demeanor when you're in truth, extremely serious.

We may assume all communication is spoken or written, but our smile, frown, handshake, and all other mannerisms are distinct modes of communication.

Put more enthusiasm — five times more enthusiasm — into your life today. Infuse your life with enthusiasm. Your team members will be excited about your ideas and suggestions. Communicate with enthusiasm. Communication is the single most central tool of empowering leadership in the creation of a team that flies together. We must understand the differences between ourselves and others to ensure we're understood and that we understand. Through enthusiastic communication, you will become fully alive while enlivening the team.

* Commit to getting the message across.

* Understand the other person.

* Empower your message with specificity.

* Admit your vulnerability and let the real you shine through.

* Put five times more enthusiasm into your communication.

Be brave enough to live life creatively

The creative is the place
where no one else has even been.
You have to leave the city of your comfort
and go into the wilderness of your intuition.
You can't get there by bus,
only by hard work and risk
and by not quite knowing what you're doing.
What you'll discover will be wonderful.
What you'll discover will be yourself.

-Alan Alda

Vision For The Voyage

"The real voyage of discovery consists not in seeking new lands but in seeing with new eyes."

-Proust

Geese embark on their annual pilgrimage instinctively. They have no choice. By contrast, the routes we humans follow are volitional. We choose the direction we take and whether to fly alone, at cross purposes, or *in formation*. The empowering leader involves everyone in the organization in creating a direction and shapes a formation so the team can enjoy the advantages geese experience naturally. Creating alignment among humans who have free will, self-interest and differing values and interests is no easy task. The team needs information about where we are headed and why we are aimed in that direction. Armed with this information, they can fly in formation. The goal is to shape a future that embraces the many seemingly diverse interests of all disciplines within the organization including engineering, sales, production, maintenance, service, accounting and marketing. The team sets its direction through a shared mission and vision. Begin with a vision.

Why Look Beyond?

Imagine you have already accomplished your vision at the highest level of excellence imaginable. How does it look, sound and feel when you walk into your organization? What has happened to morale? To communication?

Visioning is a creative process. In an executive survey, 98 percent of respondents cited a strong sense of vision as the most important attribute for a CEO in organizations for the 21st century. The vision is a stretch from what is to what can be; it is a look beyond what we currently see. The vision calls us to courageously take a risk on creating a dynamic future. Holding a vision means committing to a reality that currently does not exist. Through a vision, organizations take their collective hopes and convert them into a reality. Walt Disney said: "If you can dream it, you can do it." Visionary leaders are creators who clarify the aspirations of the team, distilling those aspirations to written words.

The vision statement is a short paragraph or two that creates a picture of a desirable future in the mind of the reader. The vision places work tasks in an inspirational perspective and moves the team past its "story" — all the reasons things cannot be done.

A vision lifts us up, calling the team to a mutually compelling future. The vision moves us through what may seem like insurmountable problems, the blockage of self-interest and tumultuous change. We move beyond our fears and begin to believe in the impossible.

Your organization's vision statement will help the team see how it can create an exciting future by building on past and present strengths. The vision statement draws people into the change effort rather than forcing them to undergo change. The empowering leader communicates a captivating, magnetizing, energizing vision, big enough to empower the entire team. The team begins to pull together toward that future. The vision supports the team through change, and transcends the ordinary into the masterful.

Organizations challenged by a meaningful vision demonstrate creativity, enthusiasm and a can-do attitude. People want to believe in the significance of their work and know they make a difference. Visionary leaders effectively link individual desires with organizational targets, thus tapping hidden reserves of commitment, talent and energy. Unleashing potential enables organizations to experience breakthrough productivity gains while enhancing individual fulfillment.

After conducting an Employee Opinion Survey for an Oregon glass manufacturing company, I could see the team lacked a clear, unifying sense of direction and purpose. We began by working with the management team to develop a vision statement for the organization. After hours of straining over every word, we had made great progress, but we still weren't completely satisfied. Two weeks later, we convened a Saturday meeting of the entire organization, about 100 people, at a suburban hotel. As a part of the Cultural Quality Awareness Day, we distributed a draft of the proposed vision statement. We formed teams of 10 people each at separate tables. We asked everyone to review the vision statement and offer suggestions for improvement. Some of the best ideas for improvement came from those in the organization who usually did not speak up. The newly improved vision statement was published in the company's new newsletter, *Lite News,* and engraved on two 4-foot by 8-foot plywood signs that were hung at the entrance of their plants. Their vision read: *An ongoing commitment to develop new and better products that exceed market standards. Provide our customers with quality products, timely and reliably delivered. Involve our employees in a safe and happy workplace with the proper tools and training. Reward honesty, hard work and integrity. Foster an environment that encourages personal growth, leadership and team commitment.*

"Quality Products By EnLITEned people!"

This vision became the litmus test for decisions over the next several months, including the decision to teach English as a second language in the evenings. This plan grew out of the vision to foster better communication and contribute to the growth of every member on the team. The vision statement also led to more involvement between departments and customers. For instance, the packaging department manager began visiting customers' sites. He had never before met a customer. Seeing how important packaging was to his customers boosted the manager's self-esteem, which in turn bolstered morale of all the workers involved in packaging, strengthening their commitment to continue making improvements.

The vision statement also guided the president to make significant financial investments in quality training. The company began to check finished glass with a diamond loop and micrometer rather than using just their naked eyes and a tape measure. This dramatically reduced the number of returns and credits for flawed glass. Within a short time, the organization's reputation for quality helped land a sale outside the declining wood products industry to the expanding high technology industry. That high-tech sale amounted to 10 percent of the glass manufacturer's annual business. It is especially amazing, considering that only a year and a half earlier, the same high tech firm would not even take calls from the glass manufacturer because of its undisciplined manufacturing processes and poor reputation for quality. And it all began with a vision.

Organizations without a clear vision statement tend to be bureaucratic, lethargic and uninspired. When management fails to provide clear direction, team members create their own direction. You may hear people say: "Don't ask me. It's not my job." or "I just work here." Such persons are territorial. They do not visualize themselves as part of a team working toward a greater good. They do their job but lack the energy and sense of urgency to go beyond their limited job description. Lack of vision results in loss of power and misdirected efforts, no matter how valiantly you have mapped out the road to increased sales and profits. "Strategic plans are worthless, unless there is first a strategic vision," says futurist John Naisbitt. Without a vision and the belief that a greater tomorrow awaits us, the human spirit disintegrates. We lack purpose.

A vision statement is more than an academic exercise. Empowered leaders recognize the long-term individual and organizational benefits of clarifying direction and uniting behind a shared purpose. A shared vision provides clarity, stimulates creativity, unites diverse individuals, and creates a passionate force that makes a profound difference.

J. Willard Marriott, Jr., Chief Executive Officer of Marriott Hotels, has sustained organizational excellence and an enviable bottom line through his strong people-development vision. On a more global scale, visionary leaders have impacted our lives: Dr. Martin Luther King, Jr., awakened the American consciousness with his statement, "I have a dream that my four little children will one day live in a nation where they will be judged not by the color of their skin, but by the content of their character."

Creating A Vision Statement

A meaningful vision statement addresses the business' necessity for change, long and short-term goals, benefits to all stake-holders (customers, suppliers, co-workers, stockholders) and the need for every person's committed participation. The vision statement states our purpose, lays the groundwork for future excellence and reflects the needs of the organization's external and internal customers. Finally, the vision statement is created in order to instill a feeling of pride among all team members as it represents their identity. You can evaluate your vision statement by the following criteria:

1. Does the vision statement include: What you do; who you serve; your desired level of quality and efficiency?

2. Does the vision accurately represent the hopes and direction of the organization?

3. Is the vision a permanent, comprehensive statement reflecting the values, culture, and environment of the organization?

4. Does the vision address all of the activities and functions of the organization?

5. Is the vision concise, clear, and understandable?

6. Is the statement presented to all members of the organization in a manner designed to promote maximum commitment?

Sometimes, it helps to be dramatic. A vision memo circulated through the office will be discarded along with the weekly reminder not to park private vehicles in the truck-loading zone. As the entire workforce of 82 employees looked on, an executive at Zidell Marine Construction rose 20 feet in the air on the front of a forklift. He tore the brown paper wrapper off a five by ten-foot plywood sign and unveiled the organization's new Vision Statement:

> **LEADING** the market with quality products from inspired people who are the best in marine construction.
> **MAXIMIZING** the utilization of our resources.
> **BUILDING** safely with integrity, skill and pride.

Just before starting to work with Zidell, a barge manufacturer in Portland, we had conducted an Employee Opinion Survey developed in conjunction with the Industrial Organizational Psychology Department at Roosevelt University in Chicago. The survey asks employees to rate their level of agreement with 36 qualitative statements, a number of which measure the degree to which people feel their organization is *in formation*. For example, team members respond to comments such as, "Teamwork among departments contributes to optimum quality and service," and "There are few service gaps between departments." A few months after developing their Vision Statement and participating in over 40 hours of leadership training, we repeated the survey. We found that teamwork effectiveness had shot up 24 percent.

Here are some additional strong Vision Statements:

Eastside Plating is the tenth largest plating and finishing company in America. The year after the creation of its vision statement, the company experienced an increase in profits for the first time in eight years. There is clear evidence of greater cooperation between departments. They even put a computer terminal at one of their client locations, which is manned by one of their own employees on a half-time basis. In spite of the fact that they have the majority of their team members tied up in training up to a half day a week, they experienced a real increase in profit.

ESP's Vision

Our ESP team is a dynamic service organization dedicated to exceeding our customers' expectations by honoring each commitment, training each employee, improving each process, and protecting our environment, we create our continuing growth and profitability.

Customer Service

Our first responsibility is to our customers. Without them, we would have no reason for being here. We strive to service a dynamic assortment of industries. Our concept of value to the customer is to give them the best combination of quality, delivery, and service at a competitive price.

* *We require that the entire organization be continuously customer focused. Our future success depends on meeting customer needs better than our competition.*

* *We recognize that we are an integral part of our customer's manufacturing cycle and our performance has a direct bearing on their success. We strive to serve our customers by providing up to date processes and technology. We will continually set up new or special pro-*

cesses as required, realizing that both parties will benefit in the end. We will responsibly process parts that our customers have entrusted to us. We are committed to meet our customer's demands.

* *We plan on constantly maintaining and improving our facilities and systems to enhance reliability and competitiveness.*

After Pro-Tech developed their vision statement some four years ago, they have increased their market share, broadened their market offerings, and improved the productivity and profits of the out-of-state plant. As their plants have been running with high profitability, they have been able to free up the president of the company to become Mayor of the town of his residence.

Pro-Tech's Vision

Our name is the standard in high-quality accessories for the trucking industry. We are in business with our customers and suppliers, developing trusting relationships through open communication, flexibility and responsiveness. We reward honesty, commitment, integrity and encourage personal growth through team management. Our continued profitability and growth contributes to the security and well-being of our team members and their families. PRO-TECH is QUALITY meeting Customer.

No one with a compelling purpose and a great vision knows exactly how it will be achieved. Be willing to follow an unknown path, allowing the road to take you where it will. Surprise, serendipity and uncertainty all lie along the path to the future. A vision is the organization's guidance system, the DNA that allows everything to work together for the organization to fly *in formation*. Your vision creates an internal reference point for making choices and connections in a complex and rapidly changing world. It endows the individual and the organization with direction to be pulled into the future. Landing a man on the moon in a decade was the vision that John Kennedy held out as an inspiring magnet pulling an entire nation to develop the technological capability for manned space flights. Vision pulls you toward the realization of a dream you may not even have dared to imagine.

Mission: The Purpose Behind the Vision

If a vision is a compelling picture that guides you toward the future, a mission provides the canvas upon which that image is created. A mission is your organization's reason for being.

I recall going to watch greyhound racing at the Multnomah Kennel Club, the Portland area's greyhound racing facility. At the gate, a lethargic young man sat on a stool, and, without even turning his head toward me, asked in a bored voice, "So, you want a program?" This left me feeling more like an imposition than a guest. The part-time tellers and cashiers acted as if they were there to fill up their schedules, socialize with their co-workers and friends and then go home.

The Multnomah Kennel Club lacked an inspiring mission. It seemed the only ones who fully understood why they were there were the greyhounds. Their mission is to catch 'Rusty' the Rabbit. Your mission statement may be just as simple. The best mission statements are easily memorized — preferably one sentence that can be placed on the bottom of a business card, letterhead or invoice to provide an instant and continual sense of purpose while answering the question: "Why? Why do we do what we do?" Your mission statement is unique to your organization. A mission statement's purpose is to fuel you, make you proud and help you decide how to direct your energy, effort, creativity and time. A mission places your work tasks in an inspiring setting. All team members need to understand the connection between the tasks they perform and the overall mission of the organization. If team members do not know the reason they do what they do, your team can never achieve the 71 percent advantage.

The president of the Multnomah Kennel Club, George Dewey, recognized this lack of purpose in the team. He was frustrated by poor morale and high absenteeism. We worked together in the development of the **WIN** program: **W**elcome, **I**nvolve, **N**ow. That is, greet or **W**elcome the customer, **I**nvolve the customer by asking a question such as "How are you today?" and act immediately. Don't just stand there. Be proactive **N**ow!

For the first time, everyone began wearing name tags so guests would know to whom they were talking. A weekly reward and recognition program was initiated. Team members received hats, buttons and other rewards for excellent customer service. A newsletter was begun to recognize the team members who provided outstanding customer service each week.

We developed and published the club's Mission Statement: "To provide a quality entertainment experience that is fun and exciting for all guests."

The results were astounding. Not only did profits increase, morale soar and turnover decrease, workers' compensation claims dropped so dramatically that the organization's insurance carrier sent the club a letter of congratulations. Two years into the program, we interviewed team leaders on camera to get a better sense of how they felt the organization had been transformed. Pete, the track race official for almost 40 years, said he was particularly pleased when he rode up the elevator and overheard a guest speak favorably about how courteously she'd been treated. That was something he had never heard before. "In the 30-some years I've worked here, I can't ever remember hearing a customer say something positive" (about customer service), Pete said.

Keith, a supervisor, was skeptical of the **WIN** program at first. "I thought if employees don't work out, just get rid of them," Keith said. Then he found that recognizing, praising, and rewarding for small improvements, rather than discharging team members, dramatically increased performance.

As Steve, another supervisor put it, when you let people know what they are doing right, "They get a real charge out of that."

The employees at the kennel club came to understand and live their company's mission. Do you know the mission of your organization? Many people answer, "To make money?" Here is the first secret of empowering leaders: Making money is not the mission of any organization — with the possible exception of the Federal Bureau of Engraving and Printing — and even that is doubtful! The Multnomah Kennel Club did increase earnings. They had the largest one-night "handel" (the amount of money bet) in the history of the club during this season. The earnings were only a by-product of positive changes the Kennel Club had initiated. Purely financially motivated organizations rarely succeed. Money is an outcome of fulfilling your mission; it's not the reason the organization exists.

Remember the phrase *A pizza in 30 minutes!*? That mission statement not only separated Domino's from every other pizza business, it defined the organization so precisely that people thought of Domino's more in the delivery business than in the pizza business. For a time, Domino's dominated the pizza business world-wide!

Your mission statement answers the questions: "In what way do we make the world a better place?" "What needs do we meet?" "What do we do better and more efficiently than others?" The mission is not something the organization moves toward, which is a goal or an objective, but rather what the organization represents, the heart of the organization. If this distinction is not absolutely clear, nothing really holds the organization together.

Together the vision and mission represent the organization's intent. They are two distinct entities. They provide guidance about our future, expressed in terms of our vision, and what we stand for, expressed in terms of mission.

The Mission Statement for Turbo Management Systems is: *Empowering Your Team to Achieve World-Class Performance.*

By contrast, the Vision Statement for Turbo Management Systems, Ltd. reads: *A world-wide organization made up of persons committed to their personal growth and to the philosophy of Turbo Management Systems, Ltd. There lives inside of us a genius, a power, a capacity — an untapped potential. This possibility for being and becoming is seen in the shadows of our past achievements — the mist of dreams and aspirations. We tap our potential by gaining confidence from our achievements, accepting responsibility for our present and committing to our dream. We provide a process for creating an empowered culture and lasting change for our client organizations.*

Those statements guide and inspire all the members in our organization as they make choices about strategies, customers, markets, products and services.

Empowering leaders concretely express the core, underlying reason the organization exists — no fluff or platitudes. Unless this common mission is clear, people will naturally veer off in different directions. When this occurs, the formation is broken, the lift of the team is lost, and the leader has missed the opportunity to empower.

The visionary organization, bent on a mission and flying *in formation*, positions itself to shape its future rather than be shaped by outer forces. Fulfilling its mission daily, while working to build a reality that does not yet exist, the visionary organization simultaneously watches the bottom line and embraces the human element. Leaders and their teams function as partners in working toward a magnetic vision of the future with an inspiring purpose. The organization actively celebrates successes and views failures as temporary setbacks, learning opportunities. Flying in "V" formation, the organization revels in each stage of the journey, never losing sight of its vision, which lies just beyond the horizon.

*** Create a vision that encompasses the
collective hopes of the entire team.**

*** Present the vision statement in an integrating,
dramatic way.**

***Replace profit as the mission,
with profit as a measure of doing things right.**

*** Ask "Why are we here? What difference do
we make?"**

*** Fulfill your mission daily and work toward a
reality that does not yet exist.**

Man in the Glass

When you get what you want in your struggle for self
And the world makes you king for a day.
Just go to a mirror and look at yourself
And see what THAT man has to say.

For it isn't your father or mother or wife
Whose judgment upon you must pass;
The fellow whose verdict counts most in your life
Is the one staring back from the glass.

Some people may think you a straight-shootin' chum
And call you a wonderful guy.
But the man in the glass says you're only a bum
If you can't look him straight in the eye.

He's the fellow to please, never mind all the rest,
For he's with you clear up to the end.
And you've passed your most dangerous, difficult test
If the man in the glass is your friend.

You may fool the whole world down the pathway of life
And get pats on your back as you pass;
But your final reward will be heartaches and tears
If you've cheated the man in the glass.

-Dale Winbrow

>>> 3

Values For The Voyage

You, who are on the road, must have a code
that you can live by.

Crosby, Stills & Nash

Profits were down at a large newsprint manufacturing mill. Competition was fierce and salaried personnel agreed to a 10 percent pay cut. I was working with the organization to bring the team in *formation* when we heard the news: The president of the organization, according to the international press, had just celebrated his birthday by chartering a yacht. He spent half a million dollars on a lavish party for himself. How do you think those team members who had just agreed to a 10 percent cut felt?

The Value Of Consistency

Loyalty cannot be bought, coerced, commanded, or manipulated. It can only be earned through a mutual respect of shared values. When the team members learned about their leader's self-indulgent party, many felt betrayed. Why should they remain loyal to an organization so blatantly hypocritical? This executive sent the message that he valued frivolity and self-indulgence far more than he did the well-being of the work force. His message could not have been more blatant had it been spelled out in a memo and stuffed in with the shrunken paychecks. Ironically, this kind of behavior cost a business far more than any savings derived from cutting wages.

In recent years, ethics in public life has received greater attention. Politicians, business people and others are being scrutinized over their ethical conduct. One reason public debate about ethics has flourished is that society realizes it no longer has to silently tolerate leaders who promise one thing then do another. Further fueling the controversy is disagreement over traditional values. This makes it extremely important for top management to behave as impeccably as possible so that the work force won't perceive a distinction between stated values and observed behaviors. Upper management has both the opportunity and the responsibility to say, "This is what we stand for. This is how we will live and be." Empowering leaders must then define the values most vital to their organization, communicate those values to all employees, and most importantly, never behave in a manner that compromises or undermines those values.

I Quit

Doug, a project manager for a major contractor, told our Leadership Development LAB that a contractor he had formerly worked for had pressured him to rejoin his firm. Doug laid out in complete detail the terms under which he would agree to work for the firm again. The contractor agreed unconditionally to the terms, including Doug's starting salary.

"A week after I returned to work for him, he informed me what my salary would be, which turned out to be about 25 percent less than our original agreement," Doug said. "He explained that I'd get a bonus at the end of the year to make up the difference. By that time it was too late for me to go back to my previous job, so I was stuck."

Five months later, Doug secured another job, leaving that contractor for the second and last time. "The lesson I learned from this experience is that those who violate trust and breech agreements, over-promise, and then under-deliver will never secure the loyalty needed to build an empowered team," Doug said. "Keep your word, be impeccably honest in all of your dealings and never let it be said, 'You better be careful; he'll promise you anything.' "

Empowering leaders devote more time earning the commitment of their team than trying to chase down and entice potential team members. It is a wasted chase if you have to entrap new people with trickery and lies. If that is your strategy, you will never build a lasting, championship team. What could this contractor have been thinking? How did he expect to get away with this? This kind of desperate action only leads to more desperation — and into a downward spiral. Pledge to lead from the highest ideals in all of your interactions. Begin today to always treat others with impeccable honesty. Tell the absolute truth in all of your dealings.

The Ethical Dilemma

Values are the codes by which we live. Values are made up of ethics and morals. Ethical conduct is different from legal conduct. Legal conduct means doing the minimum that is required under the law to avoid prosecution. Ethical conduct often demands a higher standard. Some people believe that ethical conduct should be governed by the Golden Rule, treating others as you would want them to treat you. However, not all people have the same standards about how they want, or expect, to be treated. The Platinum Rule is treating others not how you want to be treated, but how they want to be treated.

During our vacation in Alaska, my wife and I toured a non-working gold dredge #8. The dredge was launched on a man-made lake in the late 1800s. The workers sifted gold from the dredged up dirt. The pounding from the dredge was so loud that the noise could be heard in Fairbanks almost 15 miles away. Many workers lost their hearing after only four years of this arduous labor. This was not a place where workers felt tremendous loyalty. Over the years, many workers found innovative ways to steal from the company.

One technique was to grease their hair, so that as they worked through the day, they could rub gold dust in it. They would then go home, wash their hair over a bucket and pan out the gold. The guide told us about one laborer who seemed to have a severe limp, causing him to drag one foot. After the dredge had closed down, the man with the limp was spotted in Anchorage by one of his former co-workers. He was, however, not limping. The former co-worker asked how his foot had healed. The man laughed and said he had never had a limp. He had cut a hollowed out V-shape in the heel of his shoe and would drag his foot to scoop up gold dust daily.

If organizations drag their feet when it comes to clarifying and living from their highest ideals, team members may take their cues from the lowest common denominator. Beefed-up security systems are not the answer to company theft. What will deter theft is leaders who are examples of honesty, loyalty and integrity for their teams. You've got to admit, the guy with the scoop in his shoe was pretty creative. Just imagine how much his organization would have benefited, had he felt compelled to harness that creativity for the good of his team.

As humans, we lack inner programming that automatically sets us on the highest course of action. By contrast, geese and other animals instinctively behave in ways that will benefit their species. After all, what do geese know of values? Does the second goose in line take over out of the goodness of its heart when the lead goose tires ? Does the worker bee say it is pollinating for the benefit of the colony? No. They are pre-programmed. Human beings, on the other hand, are complex decision-making individuals with free will who can choose to play or not to play on the team, fly *in formation.*

Committing Values To Heart

The team must have defined, clarified, communicated *information* about its values. Values are only valuable when you know them. We once worked with an organization which had years before created a beautiful 19-page booklet stating its 15 values. These values were so important to the organization that the leaders hesitated to bring in an outsider — Turbo Management Systems. They were afraid we might present a philosophy inconsistent with their values. I respected their concern. At the first session of class with all of their team leaders present, I commented on the organization's values and asked if everyone was familiar with them. A few people even spoke up, saying they had helped create the original list. Then I said, "I will give $100 to the first person who will come forward and state the 15 values."

At that point, there was some slinking down in the chairs. Nobody volunteered. Nobody could remember the 15 values. I began reciting the values from memory: the first principle is Concern for People; the second is Provide for Opportunity and Assist in Self-Development; etc. (I had utilized mental images to help me remember the values.)

The next week at Session 2, Sandi, a class member, took it upon herself to create pictures on her computer of the 'mental stack' I used — a piggy bank to symbolize Conserve Resources; a Susan B. Anthony dollar to represent Dedication to Improvement. It was simple and enjoyable. With the aid of the visual stack, these leaders easily committed their values to memory.

The team must agree on its values, and these values must be articulated, communicated and reviewed on a continuing basis. The vision, combined with the mission and values, will create the greatest impact when they are visual, framed and displayed in prominent places throughout the organization. You can keep your values visible by printing them on laminated 3x5 cards, the back of business cards, key chains, invoices and packing slips.

Remember, even if you plate your values in gold, ethics and morals have a personal dimension. We are all filled with inconsistencies. When confronted with temptation or immobilized by fear, we may not always choose the highest path. We frequently find ourselves in the midst of an ethical dilemma; i.e., in a situation where you are contemplating going against a code of behavior that is generally agreed upon by a group to which you belong.

The purpose of every organization is to meet the needs of its customers. Your mission statement expresses the unique way you serve your customers. Your vision statement expresses your commitment to a future that is attractive in important ways. The values of your organization, if you wish to succeed and prosper, will be derived from your commitment to serve customers, both internally and externally.

We now realize that just living the example is not enough. It's important to clarify what we stand for through words. That's what our values statement enables us to do. After our values are carefully developed, it is easier for the team to understand management models and intentions. We all have the inclination to evaluate ourselves based on our intentions and others based on their behaviors.

The values of Turbo Management Systems are easily remembered. In fact, they spell REPEAT:

*R*eliability. *We agree to keep our promises. No stories, No excuses. We will not affix blame, we will solve problems. We agree to speak the impeccable truth with each other and with our customers. We speak our own truth from our experiences and feelings — "I" messages. We are willing to keep score on promises kept.*

*E*xtra Mile. *We agree to go beyond our contractual agreements. We will continually seek value-adding process improvements. We will create more value for our customer. We consistently communicate when, where and how extra mile service has been performed.*

*P*leasant Personality. *We appreciate people as our most valuable resource. We treat all complaints as valid and use this feedback for opportunity to improve program materials, systems, methods and processes. We respond to all requests with a "glad to" attitude.*

Enthusiasm. We commit to a green-light atmosphere. An optimistic world view. Honesty and integrity. We believe people want to do their best. We celebrate all successes.

Action. We will not ask people to wait. We will shorten or eliminate all lines. If we ask others to wait, we will give them choices and keep them coordinated with others in ways that make it easy to do our jobs.

Thank You. We will provide high touch acknowledgment to all our team members and clients. Appreciation. We provide feedback to all providers on their levels of service.

Here are additional value statements:

Trus Joist MacMillan
Basic Business Values

Trus Joist MacMillan is a dedicated team of creative, marketing-oriented individuals committed to meeting the needs of the customer, associate and shareholder.

This will be accomplished through strict adherence to the following list of Basic Business Values:

* *Unsurpassed Customer Service*
* *Respect for Our Associates*
* *Defect Free Quality*
* *Technological Leadership and Innovation*
* *A Reasonable Profit for Growth and for the Shareholders*
* *Integrity in Everything We Do.*

Trus Joist MacMillan has its Basic Business Value statement printed on a laminated business card so that it is readily available for reference.

Rotary International

The Four Way Test Of The Things We Think, Say Or Do:
1. *Is it the TRUTH?*
2. *Is it FAIR to all concerned?*
3. *Will it BUILD GOODWILL and BETTER FRIEND-SHIPS?*
4. *Will it be BENEFICIAL to all concerned?*

Oregon Business Media

Our Values:
* Family
* Time
* Continuous Process Improvement
* Learning
* Dialogue

* Empathy
* Integrity
* Success
* Commitment

Telecomm System, Inc.
Mission And Values

"Telecomm's continuing pursuit is to be the Standard of Excellence in the Personal Communications Industry in the Pacific Northwest.

Our employees take pride in their work. Everyone has an opportunity to contribute, learn, grow and advance based on their performance. We believe in a participatory environment that empowers everyone to act decisively with confidence. Employees are encouraged to express their concerns with an open mind and a commitment to problem-solving that continually strengthens the organization. Above all, we want to create a company where it is fun to work. Our people are committed to balancing their careers with successful personal lives. This assures that we maintain the freshness and vitality it takes to consistently deliver the quality of service our cus-

tomers have come to expect. You can use the above values to help quicken your processes for arriving at a way to successfully express yourself."

Justice

Justin, a controller for a sawmill, was faced with an ethical dilemma. The corporate manager, Doug, approached him as he was preparing the quarterly report for the head office and asked him to falsify the log inventory. He wanted him to inflate the count which would make the mill look profitable when, in fact, it had lost money.

"Doug, I can't do that," Justin said.

He responded, "I'm sorry I can't count on you for support."

Justin worried he might lose his job. He had been working overtime hoping for a promotion. Should he have agreed with Doug? After all, who would be hurt? Falsifying reports would not bankrupt the company nor put any person in jeopardy. The only person who stood to lose was Doug and only if he behaved unethically. Deep in his heart, however, Justin could not rationalize unethical behavior. He went to see the sawmill's General Manager at a time when the Logging Superintendent happened to be in his office and told them both about his conversation with Doug. Surprise! Doug had also tried to get them to falsify their record count to make the operation look profitable. Both of them had also refused to cooperate with his scheme.

About a month later, the three men wrote a memo about Doug's request to falsify inventory counts, signed it and made copies for each person's files. A few weeks later Justin had his annual performance evaluation, which required approval from Doug, who refused to give a salary increase because of his "lack of cooperation."

After repeated unreturned phone calls to Doug, Justin asked the plant manager to intervene, but he refused. Next, he wrote a long letter to Doug. He outlined his accomplishments during his first year. He told him that refusing to falsify a company report was not a good reason to refuse a well-deserved salary increase. He also sent a copy of this letter to the corporate controller.

Two weeks later, Doug was fired and Justin received his raise. Two weeks after that, he was promoted. "The lesson I learned from this experience," said Justin, "is the importance of holding my ground, sticking to my guns, doing what I know is right. When I do, ultimately I will win.

Stand firm in your beliefs in the face of opposition. The pressure will help you discover what you really believe in, who you really are. You will discover your true values. Hold on to your integrity. Never let a person manipulate you by saying, "I thought I could count on your support."

You will make genuine advancement based on solid footing. Even if it doesn't feel as if you have won at first, you will hold your head up high. Your winnings will come."'

The Basics

Some basic principles that can guide our ethical conduct are:
* Conducting business affairs with honesty, professionalism and skill.
* Providing the best value possible.
* Protecting the customers through the use of quality materials and business practices backed by integrity and service.

* Providing a workplace with high standards of safety, cleanliness and livability.
* Meeting financial obligations in a responsible manner.
* Complying with the spirit and letter of business contracts. Treating employees and suppliers with fairness and honor.
* Complying with the rules and regulations prescribed by law and government agencies for the health, safety and welfare of the community.

Ethical thinking, then, merely means considering oneself and one's firm as citizens of the business community and the whole society. Concern for others' well-being also mirrors your self-respect. This does not preclude financial success. Indeed, ethical thinking is essential to viable strategic plans.

A moral dilemma, by contrast to an ethical one, results from a situation in which guidelines for behavior do not exist. You must rely on your own needs and values as the basis for choosing a course of action. Ayn Rand's classic novel "The Fountainhead" describes one man's struggle to succeed in his chosen profession of architecture. Before his eventual triumph, this man, Howard Roark, spent most of his time working at manual labor or designing small projects.

Success could have been his early on had he designed buildings the way that critics, other architects and even some of his potential customers had wanted, but he refused to compromise his artistic vision. He valued his integrity more than wealth. Put another way, Roark refused to sell a product he did not believe in.

What do you do if you cannot respect the values of your business? Will, the owner and general manager of several auto repair shops, participated in one of our Leadership Development LABs. He told of his experience as a former shop manager at a small brake and muffler shop in Bellevue, Washington. Will had his own set of values and assumed that his employer understood his level of integrity.

"One day," he said, "I discovered, completely by accident, that my shop foreman was stealing from the company. He had developed an ingenious plan that was almost foolproof. I just stumbled across it. When I first confronted him with the facts, he was surprised, caught his breath and then he denied it completely. Finally, he backed down and admitted the theft. I was left with no other option than to terminate him immediately. I was very angry that he had been stealing from the company and lying to me. I felt let down, taken advantage of and personally violated."

To Will's astonishment, the man went over his boss' head to the company owner and, as Will put it, "told him some heart-jerking, finger-pointing story about me" and, as impossible as it seems, got re-hired.

"My boss didn't call me, didn't talk to me about my side; he didn't try to get the facts and sure didn't back me up. This really made me angry! I felt betrayed, this time by the boss; I felt like I was being Monday morning quarterbacked. I obviously was being second-guessed, as if I didn't know what I was doing."

Will said he learned a number of lessons about values from this experience. Although it is hard to be true to yourself when others around you are looking the other way, he said that now that he is an owner, he takes special care to back up his team:

— Back up your people when they've made a decision. "If I have a reason to question their actions or decisions, I ask them directly," Will said.

— Believe your team leaders know more about the situation than you do. "I try to look at the situation from their perspective," he added.

"The benefits you gain are team players who are not afraid to step out and make tough decisions. You will gain the full support of your team, building a team of decisive, innovative leaders who create and find ways to improve every day. You have real loyalty when and where it counts."

Values *In Formation*

Competition with Japanese and European companies is producing a global transformation in the culture of organizations. There is a paradigm shift taking place, a shift in the basic thoughts that drive management practices. We may, if we wish, resist these changes. High performance organizations of all kinds no longer have the whip, or the threat of disenfranchisement to force people to do what they will. High performance teams fly *in formation* voluntarily. No one can make you or your team join the migration to a new way of doing work. The leader of the organization still has the opportunity to disengage those who do not wish to be a part of the team. What has come with independence is a new kind of responsibility, a new kind of accountability. We can no longer blame the king or the captain for what does not work.

In American society today, we do value humanity and the human spirit. We place increasingly little value on force. We have made a major move away from management control toward working through others to improve processes that get results. Being a leader brings you face-to-face with value considerations. As an empowering leader, you walk the talk; you are the model. You show the way. You enroll, excite, empower, and nurture the team.

Teams function best when they agree on common principles. Religious groups know their creed and are united by their commitment to principles. Nations that function well have a constitution that clearly states the principles by which people and governments agree to live. Social unity and common purpose are created by common understanding of these principles. Organizations function best when they know and commit to their principles. You can return to your vision statement to reinforce the beliefs you hold that will contribute to furthering your vision.

One way to pinpoint current values is to find out what competitors, suppliers and customers say about your organization. Do they describe your company as fair, honest and competitive? Whatever they say can give you insight into your real values. If you do not know how your customers would describe you, find out.

Organizations move into *formation* by clarifying values and living by those values uncompromisingly. There is not one set of values for leaders and another set for those who do the drudge work. It's no different than the parents who drink to excess and then rage over the discovery that their children smoke marijuana. Organizations that establish values by which to live and then live by their values obtain the 71 percent advantage. They wing their way past those companies that surged ahead temporarily through compromise and expediency, and then remain in the lead.

* Clarify values with the team.

* Review your values continuously.

* Talk with your customers.

* Walk your talk.

* Live your values without compromise.

The Comfort Zone

I used to have a Comfort Zone
    where I knew I couldn't fail.
        The same four walls of busy work,
            were really more like a jail.

I longed so much to do the things,
    I'd never done before
        But I stayed inside my Comfort Zone
            And paced the same old floor.

I claimed to be so busy,
    with the things inside my zone.
        But deep inside I longed for
            something special of my own.

I couldn't let my life go by,
    just watching others win.
        I held my breath and stepped outside
            to let the change begin.

I took a step and with new strength
    I'd never felt before,
        I kissed my Comfort Zone "goodbye"
            and closed and locked the door.

If you are in a Comfort Zone,
    afraid to venture out,
        Remember that all winners were
            at one time filled with doubt.

A step or two and words of praise,
    can make your dreams come true.
        Greet your future with a smile,
            Success is there for you!

    -Unknown

>>> 4

Champion Change

*Sometimes we stare so long at a door that is closing that
we see too late the one that is opening.*
Alexander Graham Bell

At the fifth session of the Performance Team LAB
with a steel distribution center, the night foreman, Dave, stood
up to report on the success of his team meeting. Only he did
not look too successful. "I'm not going to kid you," he said.
"My people are really down. Morale is awful." Dave had been
allotted two minutes for his presentation, but it was clear we
needed to take whatever time was necessary to fully share his
sense of despair and disempowerment to get to the root of the
problem.

The warehouses were consolidating, and layoffs were
expected. "It's hard for me to motivate people when they know
their jobs are in jeopardy," Dave said.

I asked the general manager how many people would
be laid off. He wasn't sure. I pressed for specifics. Finally he
estimated six to eight people would lose their jobs around

Thanksgiving, just a month away. We had 20 key managers in the room that noon and began looking for a way to approach this problem with integrity.

In the end, we came up with a voluntary resignation package. In the past, salaried associates received benefits upon termination, but never before were hourly team members given this kind of benefit. The compensation package included $1,000 for training. Just as important, the team members could choose if they wished to be laid off, rather than management making the decision about who would go. One worker who left had seniority. He was someone the general manager wished had stayed. Yet, as he put it, "I slept a whole lot better knowing we made this change with integrity."

This was one of many major changes implemented by the organization. In the months to come, the company set sales records again and again. Its safety record improved. Its return on investment increased by 22 percent.

Cultural Change

Change is not easy. It can produce a common side effect: a pathology of helplessness. People feel vulnerable, as if they have little influence, and begin to act like victims. Whenever people feel disempowered, commitment becomes diluted.

In order to ensure their enthusiastic participation, team members need to know how change will benefit them — the old "What's in it for me?" consideration. They need to trust that the journey, which may prove arduous at times, is worth the effort they're about to expend. They also require a road map for the journey and an understanding of their respective roles and responsibility for making change occur. Finally, every person who embarks on this journey needs to know what the end result will look like and how to recognize success when they see it.

We face the challenge of seeing our work and our organization in a world-wide context. For a team to move into higher levels of performance, everyone in the organization must approach change with self-confidence. In other words, we must be willing to step out of our comfort zones. Creating the ideal formation may require a fundamental change in your organization. Change is an opportunity, not a threat. Real change is not tweaking; it means stripping things down to their core and asking, "Do we really get value out of this activity?" Re-focus the roles of management and supervision; modify incentive systems; and capitalize on the untapped reservoir of team members' ideas for improvement. Empowering visionary leaders embrace change. We can live with change successfully if we know where we stand with our values, vision and mission. If we know that even though our roles may change, our mission and reason for being remains intact. As Bill Goebel, President, Zidell Marine, put it: "Our competition is not standing still; our competition, around the corner and around the world, is continuously reading, meeting, studying, improving. You must get better, measurably better, to stay; even much better to get ahead."

DS x MV x FS > RC

To bring about meaningful change, you must have "DS," Dissatisfaction with the Status quo; multiplied by "MV," a positive Magnetic Vision of the way we imagine things can be, a passion for the possible; multiplied by "FS," First Steps we take toward action. Taking action dispels fear, builds trust and confidence. The product of these three must be greater than "RC," the natural Resistance to Change.

A critical mass of the organization must be discontent with the status quo, see a common vision of a preferred future and agree on first steps that will move the organization toward a more powerful *formation*. We resist change because we find security in the familiar. The toughest leg of the journey is letting go, abandoning the comfort of the familiar, and thus freeing ourselves of old ways that inhibit our progress. Few of us willingly abandon established patterns of doing things only because someone shows us reasons to change.

In order for change to occur, we must be dissatisfied with what we are experiencing now and have a clear vision of what will be more rewarding. We must take the steps that will move us forward. Dissatisfaction can spring from the fact that we are not competing successfully. We are not winning new customers. Profits are shrinking. We grow increasingly frustrated as scrap piles grow or as customers turn to the competition. If you are discontent and lack "MV" or "FS," you will become frustrated. If you possess a vision, but feel no discontent, you will grow wistful and remain passive. With any of the three elements missing, you remain static. The status quo has a survival instinct and can be stronger than the desire for change. It is not enough to identify the dissatisfaction and create the vision. You must commit and take meaningful action steps.

After years of watching management teams fail at taking well-intentioned action steps, I realized we had to stretch beyond conventional means in helping our clients break through the status quo. We had to create conscious shock, a real intervention. We began facilitating a peer evaluation process with management teams using the Management Team

Advance program. Each person fills out a survey on each team member in order to provide all individuals on the management team with a profile of themselves as seen through their peers' eyes. At one such meeting for an organization that rents scissors-lifts to construction companies, the managers read their profiling feedback over lunch. When they returned, they were surprised to see a video camera set up in the room. Each manager then in turn asked the team how they could improve their contribution to the organization. The managers then came up with suggestions for each of their peers. They may have been a little upset to read what their peers thought of their management prowess. They realized, perhaps for the first time, that their peers viewed them as indecisive, poor delegators, impatient listeners or ineffective planners. As they got into the spirit of the process, they genuinely sought and received constructive feedback to create breakthroughs in communication and teamwork. We jointly created a "Magnetic Vision" for breakthrough performance for each manager, and then we videotaped each manager's three-step action plan.

One of the organization's biggest problems had been failing to share scarce resources. A branch in one city would call another in search of a certain size lift. Usually the manager would look in the lot, see the needed lift and say, "Nope, we don't have any right now" or "All of ours are spoken for." The feedback session created a renewed commitment to truly cooperate in reducing competition and increasing cooperation between branches. Over the next year, the organization set sales and profit records.

A Change for the Better

A great deal of time is devoted to non-productive activities, such as writing reports that are never read, slapping Band-Aids™ on recurring problems, forcing compliance to policies and procedures that no longer work, or playing internal political games. Talented people who might otherwise soar instead wear themselves out flapping their wings just to remain aloft.

There are people who enjoy achievement (always adapting in order to achieve), those who need control (adapting in order to take the reins), and those who simply want to earn a decent living in order to enjoy a personal life. The latter group comprises the vast majority of the population, and it is the potential contribution of this group that organizations most frequently squander. The *in formation* organization is sufficiently flexible to allow people who just want to earn a living to provide ideas and make decisions without putting themselves at risk physically, emotionally or financially. Persons in this group frequently flinch at risk-taking because they do not want to propose anything that they perceive might threaten their position. They may see errors and know a simple, fast way to correct them, but hesitate to speak up because they know all too well the rigidity of the structure. They anticipate either trouble for themselves or ridicule from others. They wonder, "Why bother?"

Some organizations "resist." The people who make up the organization seem to be at war internally with those in their own business environment. A "we/they" attitude permeates the organization, labor vs. management, department "A" vs. department "B," senior staff vs. junior staff. The client becomes lost in the shuffle. Naming, blaming, shaming, fault finding, and turf and tail protection divert creativity away from productivity and goal attainment. Controls, procedures, regulations, mechanisms and "this is the way we have always done things" function as effective barriers to empowerment. Resistors tend to argue for and, therefore, achieve their limitations. These organizations seem to have lost their mission, their vision, their spirit — and their future.

What the maintaining and resisting organizations have in common is an allergy to change. By contrast, the *in forma-tion* organization is sufficiently flexible to embrace change. The use of human resources in an *in formation* organization is dynamic and productive at every level, with a focus on continuous improvement. When a choice is required between doing the right thing and doing things right (i.e., according to policy), in an *in formation* organization people choose doing the right thing with no fear of punishment. Team members willingly take risks for the sake of the organization. People are linked in a common bond of clarity of purpose and unity of direction. Les Schwab has created a retail tire sales empire by truly believing in people and focusing on "Pride in Performance." Apple Computer enthusiastically supports creative thinkers for developing user-friendly products. A "passion for the possible" vision influences internal and external forces in creating results that count.

When implementing change, consider the following:
1. **Provide Freedom.** When you don't, people seek it (almost always resulting in counterproductive behavior), and we call them poor performers. When you do provide freedom, they are responsible. Teach, and let them grow and develop.
2. **Provide Safety.** When you don't, people seek it, and we say they're being defensive. They are simply pro-

tecting themselves. When you provide safety, people are willing to learn and risk. Let them teach you.

3. **Provide Attention.** When you don't, people seek it, and we call them problematic or selfish. When you pay attention to them, they are attentive in return and can share. Let them share with you.

Helping all your leadership teams facilitate change will make it easier to bring your entire team *in formation.* Always keep a picture in mind of the way things will be and work toward that vision. Ralph Waldo Emerson said, "It is one of the most beautiful compensations of this life that no man can sincerely try to help another without helping himself."

Quality Steering Team

The Quality Steering Team will help guide the change effort, ensuring greatest use of all resources and consistent effort. The Quality Steering Team is made up of a rotating cross section of the organization. Its function is to facilitate the change effort and provide overall direction and resources. The team addresses the planning of the change strategy and monitoring of progress, including, as appropriate, the implementation of action steps. The Quality Steering Team must provide continuity and long-term support to ensure consistent effort in areas where individuals may let up. The team distributes responsibility, so the quality improvement effort does not depend on just one person. Major change efforts require time and continuity of leadership for success.

In addition to distributing responsibility, the steering team has symbolic value. It communicates a serious commitment to something new and different. This team plans the change strategy to fit your culture and monitors how change efforts are progressing. As implied by the title, it steers the process to assure the highest level of involvement in and acceptance of the planned changes.

The performance team concept will only succeed if good, solid training is developed and provided. The Quality Steering Team analyzes training needs and coordinates with appropriate resources to determine what new skills are required for team members to achieve their potential.

Recognition programs may need to be established or reconfigured. Tracking systems that monitor programs may be needed. The Quality Steering Team is constructed to be a ready receptacle of *information* from all sectors of the organization and its suppliers and customers. The team keeps the organization informed of successes, challenges, goals and motives through posted minutes, newsletters, electronic mail or any other appropriate means as the change process proceeds. The Quality Steering Team is the eyes, ears and mouth of the organization.

In the early stages, your organization's Quality Steering Team will meet weekly to be coached by an outside Quality Coordinator. As time goes by and there is greater maturity within processes, monthly meetings may be all that is required.

Effects of Change

Change affects individual members of the organization in different ways.

Many team members may feel uneasy about the new jobs they have to learn. One way to ease this discomfort is to have everyone put forth an extra effort to train others on their jobs and answer any questions they may have to help them learn faster. We all remember how tough it is to learn a new job, so the more supportive we are, the sooner people will feel better about their new role in the performance team culture.

Some team members may not be comfortable working with others. There are those who are loners by nature and may feel anxious about working more closely with others. Again, make the environment as supportive as possible, and this person may just wind up liking the performance team concept better than the old "go it alone" approach.

Some team members may resist the team concept itself. Most resistance occurs when the big picture is unclear. It is natural to resist when you have only a fuzzy vision of the future and your role in it. The best way to confront this resistance is through education.

* Learn as much about team members as possible.
* Learn as much about your new roles and responsibilities.
* Persist in asking questions until all *information* has been provided.
* Ask about the future of the work area and how you fit.
* Talk about your team and how to improve it.
* Enlist the support of your performance team members to help shape the team productively.
* Partake in the planning and direction of the team by taking on the team's administrative duties. Your involvement helps reduce natural resistance.

As stated earlier, some people resist cultural change because they cannot picture themselves in the future. If you can envision how teams will operate, you can modify the environment accordingly for the changes ahead. In the performance team environment, every member is expected to work within the team. In other words, the productivity of the team will be determined by how well the members work together.

Mastering The Forces Of Change

History illustrates that cultures enter periods of transformation when they clash with another culture or when they must compete. The clash between the East and West during the Christian Crusades led to a transformation that became the Renaissance in Western Europe. This cultured transformation led to the embracing of new ideas, enhanced awareness and appreciation of art, as well as new organizational structures.

Today we are in the midst of a renaissance in the life of Western organizations. This renaissance is the result of competition and a clash with an Eastern culture, but this time it is the result of commercial rather than military competition. Competition with Japanese and European companies is producing a global transformation in the culture of organizations. There is a paradigm shift taking place, a shift in the basic thoughts that drive management practices.

Although we may resist at first, as time passes, we become used to the new state of affairs and we begin to perceive a glimmer of opportunity. Understanding this common "down then up" sequence of reactions will help you to implement change. When managers introduce what they see as an obviously worthwhile new procedure, person, position or piece of equipment, they often expect the change to be welcomed without hesitation. When trainers present new ideas and methods, they usually expect what they teach to be seen immediately by the learners as worthwhile and useful.

Unfortunately, both are often disappointed. Why? At first, it's not the content of innovation that matters, it is people's attitudes toward the change. To illustrate this point, please do the following:

1. On the line below, write the word "attitude" with your dominant hand.

---

2. On the line below, write the word "attitude" with your other hand.

When you look at the word "attitude" written by your non-dominant hand, you see a picture of the kind of attitude we usually have when trying to do something new. Did it feel awkward to write that way? You could not write automatically. You may have strained with each letter. The end result may look a little peculiar as well. We feel awkward and incompetent, forcibly removed from our familiar comfort zone.

Therefore, you cannot just throw something new at people, regardless of its evident value. We must assist and support people until they get through that initial period until the benefits of the new become evident. When your organization implements change, watch for these phases:

1. *Denial.* This is the stage of shock. The reality of the change has not set in. Although there is a sense of loss among team members for the old ways, productivity does continue temporarily. This causes managers to believe the transition has been accomplished. This is especially true if motivational speakers have pushed employees to make the leap.

2. *Resistance.* We often describe who we are by what we do. When asked to talk about ourselves, we spit out our job title. Since we often identify ourselves with what we do,

learning something new can make us uncomfortable. We have learned over the years how to be the best at what we do. When someone tells us we should be learning something new, it is natural to resist. In the resistance phase, strong feelings about the change emerge, such as self-doubt, anger, depression, anxiety, frustration, or uncertainty. Team members often feel sorry for themselves, thinking, "This isn't fair" or "Oh, poor me." Productivity slips, and negativity abounds. This stage is characterized by anger brought on by a feeling of helplessness. Some want to leave the organization. This is also the stage where some people do not accept the change, but merely tolerate it. They go through the motions in a very apathetic, unproductive manner, saying "Oh well, what's the use?" In order to safely weather this phase, associates must be allowed to express negativity. Creativity diverts to shooting down ideas and creating roadblocks even when change is obviously necessary.

Group rituals such as award ceremonies and celebration parties help people share their experiences and thus weather the passage. People will reach low points on the change cycle at different rates, but eventually most will shift to the up curve.

3. *Exploration.* During the exploration phase, people draw upon their internal resources and creativity to figure out their new responsibilities and to visualize their future. This can be an exciting time when people take on the change as an adventure and form powerful new bonds with their fellow pioneers.

4. *Commitment.* At this point, people are ready to make stable, long-range plans and to act on them. "Okay, this is a reality. What can I do to make it work for me?" This is the stage in which the individual accepts the change, and then

attempts to work through it in a positive way. Team members willingly re-create their mission, roles, and expectations. This phase usually lasts until the next cycle of change begins.

Without change, organizations stagnate. At any given time, people on your team will be in one of these phases of change, and you need to be sensitive to which phase they are experiencing. Try to move toward the final phase of Commitment as quickly as possible. People can go through these phases in a matter of minutes, or seemingly, millenniums. The degree to which they are involved in the decision to change and how much *information* they have in advance will greatly impact the time needed to absorb the change. Empowering leaders manage change by mentoring their teams and involving them in the change process as early as possible.

* Remember the equation of change:
DS x MV x FS > RC.

* Don't blame team members who fail to
change;
re-examine your environment.

* Implement a Quality Steering Team.

* Anticipate team members' concerns regarding change.

* Master the forces of change by recognizing
the phases.

Managing Versus Leading

Managing	Leading
Individual	Team
Fickleness	Commitment
Doing My Job	Customer Focused
Finance Focus	Production Focus
Dollars	Things and Ideas
Sales Focus	Marketing Focus
Printed or Spoken Word	Diagram Oriented (Visual)
Single Function	System
Seat of Pants Opinion	Statistical Thinking
Fragmented (Single Focus)	Holistic (Integrated)
Deductive	Inductive
Short Range/Long Range	Long Range
Activity Focus	Process Focus
Debate/Conversation	Planning/Action
Reaction	Prevention
Blame	Help
Orders	Participation
Just-In-Case	Just-In-Time
Management Control	Leadership
Technology/Machines	Human Resources
Bureaucratic	Entrepreneurial
Supplier Adversaries	Supplier Partnerships
Compartmentalized	Cooperation
Quality=Problem	Quality=Solution
Control	Breakthrough
Fire Fighting to Preserve --Status Quo	Continuous Improvement

>>> 5

Longing For Belonging

*In the 21st Century organization,
the team is the competitive weapon.*
Rosabeth Moss Kanter, Harvard Professor

I had lunch with the general manager of a computer manufacturer headquartered in Hong Kong. The organization has made copy machines for many years and then began a line of mid-size personal computers for business. After only one year, the corporation shut down the computer division because sales goals were missed by two months. Just two months! This was sad for me, because the president and general manager are good friends of mine. The sales manager, along with the rest of the sales management team, had refused to participate in our training. This was indicative of an overall lack of team cooperation between the sales department in Portland and the production department in Nashville. Here is a clear example of what losing the 71% advantage can cost you!

Something in our genetic code causes us to enjoy the game. When we form groups, know the game, know the score, and feel that we can make a difference, we strive to do our best. There have been virtually hundreds of scientific studies that demonstrate that human beings function better and learn best in groups. We are more likely to achieve personal satisfaction and motivation when working in a socially cohesive group. Isolation transforms the human spirit into a counterforce instead of one that has a great capacity for caring and collaborating with others. Isolation destroys human energy and results in frustration.

As we move from the industrial age to today's *information* age, we are learning that the most competitive high performance organizations are those that openly share *information* successfully. Those high performance organizations have opened up all lines of communication so everyone can fly *in formation*. The age of the power broker, the person who hoarded *information* and doled it out on an 'as needed' basis, is quickly fading.

We are at the point now where all team members must understand the customers' requirements, the organization's goals, strategies, vision and values, and the economic realities of risk capital. All team members have the right to know the contributions they make to the bottom line. Is this easy? No! But the pay-offs can be dramatic.

For us to create a high performance learning organization, we must share freely all *information* throughout the organization and create an environment of trust so that everyone feels free to present new ideas. *Information* allows us to move from command and control to self-directed commitment. The empowering leader must ensure that all team members have the *information* they need on key indicators to perform at the highest levels possible. We must move past the 'I don't know' to the certainty and confidence of the 'I do know.' We can only achieve the 71 percent advantage by knowing where we are now, where we are going and the part each of us play in reaching that destination. As we move at ever faster rates of speed, as targets and roles change at rocket rates of speed, we give up the security and certainty of a rigid structure. Our world is fluid and flowing. The only thing that holds us together in this fluid world is *information.*

Three Basics Of A Performance Team

1. Interactions — Performance Team members interact regularly as a natural part of their work.
2. Accountability — Performance Team members accept accountability for their output, their work. Their customers hold them accountable.
3. Processes — Performance Team members all work within the same process; i.e. a maintenance team in an oil refinery is made up of a group who have similar skills and perform within the same area; the accounting team is made up of people who work on accounts payable.

The lifeline of a performance team is *information.* The moment the team fails to receive meaningful, accurate, timely *information*, it flies off in scattered directions. Performance teams must first have *information* about the vision— where they are headed; the mission — why they exist, how they make a difference; and a set of clearly defined values. They will come to know that the old hierarchical structures and authoritarian style is being replaced by an engaged committed team.

When American organizations became aware of the importance of improving quality, many implemented quality circles and problem-solving task force groups. We heard that Japanese companies used quality circles and they were easy to adopt. Quality circles are volunteers who select a problem, endeavor to find a solution and champion its implementation. Managers approve their recommendations and are often left with the burden of implementing recommendations from many different quality circles.

We now understand that to achieve continuous improvement, we must do much more. Everyone must be involved in Performance Teams. Your organization comprises many performance teams. They receive input from suppliers and perform work tasks that create state changes and added value. These performance teams then pass their finished work on to their internal or external customers. Performance teams accept responsibility for managing their achievements. They ease the burden of managers. They are empowered to make decisions and act to improve their work process. Performance team members are the world's greatest experts in their work, their processes, and therefore, the experts on improving those processes. As on a football, basketball or baseball team, performance teams have a common interest, common scores and a common goal.

Moving Toward Team Spirit

A seismic shift is taking place in thinking about management. The major move is away from management as controller to working through performance teams that accept responsibility for continually improving their processes. Historically, the manager took responsibility for meeting customer expectations and keeping score. Today, the most successful organizations know those responsibilities belong to performance teams. Having the team accept responsibility for the quality of its work, rather than the boss, is a big change. It is important that the team process be understood as a paradigm shift, a change in basic assumptions about organizations world-wide. Team process is the key factor in quality improvement. Environments that motivate people to peak performance are not environments of high outer-control, but are environments of high self-control. Quality improvement occurs when people commit to serving their customer and continuously improving their work processes.

High performance teams have eliminated the word "try" from their vocabulary. They realize that to succeed they must commit to continuous improvement. Once a commitment is made to a fellow team member or down stream customer, they do not "try" to keep it; they keep it.

As you will discover throughout *In formation*, performance teams:
 * Are Customer-Focused
 * Plan Action
 * Share *Information*
 * Manage Performance
 * Measure Performance
 * Set Goals
 * Conduct Training
 * Take Responsibility
 * Motivate and Involve
 * Reward
 * Coach
 * Correct Mistakes
 * Solve Problems
 * Conduct Meetings

Work becomes more interesting when team members understand the whole process, and learning new jobs makes work more challenging and exciting. Once members have mastered the process, the performance team can collectively begin to solve problems and continuously improve the outputs. It also makes working on routine jobs more interesting when team members have someone else with whom to collaborate. Team members feel challenged as they perform new duties outside of the traditional aspects of their jobs, such as facilitating meetings, keeping score, working in problem-solving groups and performing team administrative tasks.

With performance teams, every team member is more valuable because each person has knowledge of several jobs instead of only one. If a job becomes automated or eliminated, you still have options. The other advantage of knowing several jobs is that you learn more about the entire process and can be more helpful when solving problems and making suggestions for improvement.

Functions of a Performance Team

The performance team manages its own activities, from ordering in-process materials to solving any interpersonal problems with team members. The performance team ensures that its members are trained properly and have the resources to complete their work and strive for continuous improvement. The following are key attributes of a performance team:

1. Reasonably Sized.
Performance teams range in size from three to 30. The most common size is about six.

2. Clearly Defined.

Performance teams define the requirements of their work to satisfy their customers. They survey customers to ensure that they understand what they consider superior performance.

3. Responsible.

Performance teams accept responsibility for the planning and production of a whole product or process, or a whole sub-assembly in the case of a complex product.

4. Studious.

Performance teams study and improve their work process. Most quality problems are the result of poor work systems or processes. The team is responsible for its own work process, defining, analyzing and improving it.

5. Score-Keeping.

Performance teams develop and monitor scores of their performance. What team performs well without knowing the score? It is natural for teams to gain satisfaction from knowledge of their performance. This is true in athletics and in business. Once the team has listened to their customers and studied their work process, they will have little trouble identifying measures of their performance.

6. Problem-Solving.

Performance teams solve problems and set goals. There is always a problem. The problem is how to improve performance and quality. Improvement will continue forever as the team identifies opportunities for the betterment of processes, sets new goals and develops action plans.

7. Action-Oriented.

Performance teams are responsible for their work and can make decisions to improve their process. They do not merely submit recommendations to someone else for approval. It is from the implementation of their ideas that the teams gain greater knowledge. This knowledge results in higher levels of performance and further efforts to improve.

8. Skillful.

Performance teams require members who are multi-skilled in their technical abilities to carry out tasks. They need a relatively high level of interpersonal skills such as communicating, conflict resolution, making group decisions, and problem-solving. They also need administrative skills in managing meetings and performing whatever administrative responsibilities are assigned.

9. Time-Conscious.

Performance teams may meet daily, weekly or as needed to coordinate work, solve problems, handle interpersonal issues or perform administrative tasks. There is usually some blend of regular formal and informal meetings as required.

Benefits Of Performance Teams

Motivation

Why do we enjoy playing on teams? Why do children naturally become excited about being on a baseball or basketball team? Teams celebrate success together, suffer their losses together, and form bonds of friendship around the activity of the team. Teams have fun because they have common goals, keep score, and gain the satisfaction of success. Team members naturally motivate one another to perform to the best of their ability.

Improved Communication

The performance team process involves everyone in the organization. Teams are forums for communication; the group shares vital *information*, discusses, asks questions and clarifies decisions together. A question is often asked by one person that is on the minds of many. Efficiency and morale are improved when members of the team have the same *information* and feel that it is being shared freely.

A Sense of Belonging

There is a special sense of group power in meeting a goal or winning a competition as part of a team. The Performance Team provides an opportunity to contribute particular strengths to the larger group and learn from the strengths of others. One of the sometimes overlooked advantages of building a championship team is "everyone wants to be on a winning team." Performance Teams solve one of your most persistent, challenging problems — staffing. People will knock on your door, seek you out and remain and grow with the organization.

Improved Quality

The first focus of Performance Teams is identifying their customers and finding ways to improve service to those customers. Quality is anticipating, conforming to, or exceeding the customer's requirements. Quality may be on-time delivery, reliability, performance within specifications, courtesy or responsiveness.

Enhanced Creativity

To compete successfully, an organization must continually find ways to do things better. Success does not come from standing still. Finding better ways is a result of human creativity. Groups of people exchanging ideas openly, listening to each other, and working toward a common goal stimulate one other to come up with new and better ideas.

Stages Of Performance Team Development

Forming, Storming, Norming, Performing

The family is the first building block of society. It is the first social structure to which we all belong. Our years of greatest learning occur when we are most dependent on the support of our parents. As we mature, we play with other children. The sharing, problem-solving and cooperation of playing are the natural learning environments for future tasks. As teenagers, we participate in teams, social clubs, groups or gangs, and we practice working together for mutual benefit, support and feelings of success. Like a growing child, a growing team has needs that change over time. You have probably experienced the strong emotions people feel during any major organizational change. Anticipation, fear, anger, acceptance and renewed self-confidence, roughly in that order, affect both the individual and the team as a whole. Understanding the phases that a growing team goes through can help you and your team members weather the confusion that comes with any serious change.

Forming

Forming is the first stage of team development. When individuals form a group, they must resolve issues before accomplishing any work. During this discovery phase team members become familiar with individual behaviors. The performance teams have to deal with many task issues. Team members may not be sure of their new roles. They are very uncertain about how to increase quality and productivity. In the Forming stage, team members want to know, "What is expected of me?" "How do I fit in?" "What are the rules?" No one feels secure enough to be genuine. Open conflict is rare. The team needs to develop operating guidelines that enhance interaction.

Storming

In this stage, team members become more comfortable with one another. They learn how to talk to each other. This is the communication stage. It begins after the members become acquainted and feel team spirit, empowered and independent of their leader. As team members begin to trust and express opinions, disagreement and conflict inevitably arise. Team members may exhibit rebellion, questioning, and impatience. This is the 'adolescent' phase. Characteristics of the storming stage are poor productivity and quality, weakened leadership and an environment of tension. This can be an unpleasant time. Typical productive behaviors are searching and differing as members communicate opinions and feelings. Typical unproductive behaviors are attacking the person rather than the problem, defending, and blaming other team members.

During the second phase, enthusiasm usually gives way to frustration and anger. Team members struggle to work together, and everything seems awkward. You will see resistance, wrangling, hostile sub-groups, jealousies, and general disgust with the transition Quality Steering Team. Ground rules may easily be disregarded.

The Team Leader can:
1. Identify and remind the team of key productive behaviors.
2. Give team members feedback on their behavior.

3. Encourage communication and interaction.
4. Discuss realistic goals for the team.
5. Act as a boundary manager.

Norming

This stage occurs after the team has learned to work effectively as a team, solving problems and developing competence. This is the productivity phase. After discovering the worth of individuals, the team begins to set realistic objectives. The team can now solve problems by utilizing the problem-solving process and the highest skills and abilities of each team member.

Team members' relationships have improved greatly by the norming stage. Typical productive behaviors are valuing team members' opinions and acting as a single unit. Typical unproductive behaviors are complacency (as the team becomes too sure of itself) and forgetting that problem-solving requires analyzing all facts and data. The team must remember its job is to continually improve both the environment and its outputs.

Gradually, the team gains balance and enters the tranquil 'norming' phase. People find standard ways to do routine things, and they drop the power plays and grandstanding. The main danger now is that team members hold back their good ideas for fear of further conflict.

What the leader can do:
1. Facilitate the use of problem-solving and decision-making processes.
2. Help the team focus on its performance data.
3. Provide positive reinforcement for success.
4. Help the team effectively organize an action plan.

Performing

This is the ultimate stage of the Performance Team's development where it responds automatically to challenges. The team has a clarity of purpose and a sense of unity, and flies *in formation*. Performance Team members know each other, solve problems and make decisions comfortably and without fear. Effective communication keeps each team member informed of the current level of job performance. A high level of energy is evident.

Relationships in the work group are extremely positive at this stage. Everyone respects the other group members and can now give and receive constructive feedback about how they interact and carry out their jobs. Conflict between members is not avoided, it is settled.

In this fourth and final phase, the team goes about its business with smooth self-confidence. By now, people have learned to disagree constructively, compromise, and apply their full energy to a variety of challenges. It's important to note that reaching the performing phase does not mean smooth sailing forevermore. A team can experience a stormy period at any time – e.g., when it's under unusual pressure. The team can also return to its forming phase if it adds or loses members. If the team begins to recycle through earlier phases, the team must find its balance and settle down to business. The leader can:

1. Act as team member.
2. Allow the team to function independently.
3. Rotate team leadership.
4. Serve as a consultant/advisor.
5. Encourage and reinforce team success.
6. Serve as a catalyst for continuous improvement.

Regular team meetings help organizations implement quality improvement. When performance teams meet, they are not meeting to decide if there is a problem. Rather, they are meeting to review their ongoing work performance and goals, and discuss ways to improve.

You create breakthroughs to new levels of performance when you capture the collective genius of every member of your team and move into formation.

* **Remember the basics of performance teams: processes, interactions, and performance.**

* **Empower teams by putting them in charge.**

* **Performing teams keep score, solve problems and take action.**

* **Expect enhanced motivation, communication and creativity.**

* **Anticipate the four stages: forming, storming, norming, performing.**

Reason

Reason...
   Everyone wants one, I suppose.
A reason to exist.
A reason to be.
A reason that grows,
The stimulus for action,
      to move past self-satisfaction.
That is what the customer is for me.
And when I strive to make them smile,
I exceed my best by a mile.
And so I say...
      Thank you for the customer.
Who demands my very best,
      They keep me on my quest.

-Larry W. Dennis, Sr.

$$>>> 6$$

Customer Commitment

*If your focus is on serving your customer, you won't have
to worry about beating the competition.
There won't be any.*

Henry Ford

Shirt Off Your Back

At the end of a full day, I arrived at Salishan Lodge,
a resort on the Oregon Coast. I had packed in a hurry, really
just threw some things in a suitcase, and ran out the door.
Donna Lee, my wife, had left earlier for a meeting. Although
you would think I would be able to pack on my own, I have
never quite mastered Donna Lee's knack for packing exactly
what I need for a trip.

After checking into my room, I began to unpack. Uh-
oh! No dress shirt! What do I do? I had an important meeting
scheduled at the crack of dawn, and all the coast stores were
closed by this time. I called my associate's room to see if he
had an extra shirt. No luck. I called to see if the Salishan gift

shop sold dress shirts. No luck. I talked to the night manager, and she told me what I already knew: "Everything's closed, and nothing will be open until 9:00 or 10:00 tomorrow morning." I told her my dilemma.

I said, "I'll bet you'll come up with some way to help me out."

Her response was, "Well, I'll sure try."

A few minutes later, she called back, "By the way, what size are you?" she asked.

"I wear a 16-34."

About 10 minutes later, she called back again, "We found one of the bellman's shirts in your size. It's here at the front desk ready for you." The following morning I arrived at the front desk dressed in everything but my shirt and tie. They held up three white dress shirts from which to choose.

Salishan has always enjoyed a positive reputation. I have conducted many programs and seminars there over the years. I like the resort's retreat-like setting and fireplaces in the rooms. Still, the truth is, I am more impressed with the three white dress shirts than any hotel amenity. The free shampoo and terry cloth bathrobe are great, but how can anything possibly compare that to a place that literally offers you the shirt off its back?

In the increasingly competitive 21st century, when our customers are expecting more than ever, you will find ways to create market distinction and strategic relationships with clients in order to survive. Most alert managers know they must be more competitive and more customer-driven than ever before. Ways must be found to reduce errors and shorten cycle time. There is a risk of failure if ways to help your customers are not found. Customers need to believe that you are willing and able to give them the shirt off your back.

Identifying The Customer

Who are our customers? What are their expectations? How do we exceed our customers' expectations? How can we measure and keep score on expectations met? A customer is anyone, outside or inside your organization, to whom you provide products or services. This differs from the traditional definition. We tend to think of the customer solely as the person or organization that pays for what we deliver. Under this new definition, anyone you provide service to is a customer. For example, if you are the boss on a construction site, the foremen and estimators provide you with products and services. Therefore, they need to know what you view as quality and excellence. In turn, you provide them the best quality delegation, materials, tools and team members to get the job done. Customer orientation is achieved when all individuals think of themselves as suppliers to others within the organization, serving these internal customers as well as the traditional external customer, as well as the sense of being a team member contributing to the total end product.

All decisions made must be built around the question, "How will this affect the customer?" In a factory, the internal customer process can be easily seen. As parts come down the assembly line, every person adds something to the item and passes it along to the next "customer." Every team creates state changes that add value for the down-stream customer.

For a simple example of the internal customer concept, consider how orders are processed in a nursery:

1. After an order is received, the sales department becomes the customer of the person who receives the order.

2. The sales department then passes the order along to the production expediter. Sales are then the providers, and the production expediter is the customer.
3. The production expediter then passes the order along to the job foreman. At this point, the expediter is the provider and the foreman is the customer.
4. This process, of course, continues until the ultimate external customer's orders are completed to their satisfaction.

Organizations need to understand what it is about them, their products and their services that their customers value, and where their customers believe they could receive more value if the organization did things differently.

In order to provide superior customer service, every team member must understand both the function of business in general and the function its organization performs for its customers. Customer value can be illustrated by the following formula:

$$\text{Customer Value} = \frac{\textbf{What the Customer Gets}}{\textbf{What it Costs the Customer}}$$

This equation includes all aspects of what the customer receives and what it cost them in time, effort, money and frustration. The real cost of poor quality is rarely calculated. When it is, the results are startling. For example, during a single year, faulty checks accounted for about one-half of all check-processing costs in United States banks; also a recall of radial tires at a major manufacturer cost the company more than the organization's net income for that year.

Quality, safety and efficiency are values that drive your quality improvement efforts. Yet, of all the rallying cries we have at our disposal, the most powerful is the customer. All of us are customers. We all have experienced what it feels like to be treated royally, and we have all experienced the disgust, frustration and anger of shoddy service. Place yourself in the customer's shoes as you strive for excellence.

Each organization is a series of internal suppliers and customer teams. A performance team receives input that it uses to produce the goods or services for which it is responsible. The input suppliers can include specification, orders, *information*, decisions, money or the actual product. The team that receives the input from its supplier is a customer of that supplier team.

The team receiving input from its suppliers is also a supplier to another team within the organization. This relationship exists throughout the organization. Each team that supplies goods and services to either an internal or external customer should continuously attempt to discover the expectations of its customers and strive to exceed those expectations.

One of the keys to the success of the Japanese auto companies has been an enhanced relationship between themselves and their suppliers. For example, Honda Manufacturing in Marysville, Ohio, has dedicated suppliers within the 50 mile radius of their plant. The Stanley Company supplies the headlight and taillight assemblies. They make deliveries several times a day, minimizing or eliminating inventory in both plants. (Japanese companies have an average two-hour inventory, where many American companies have two weeks of inventory.) When a defect is discovered, Stanley has knowledge of the defect in no more than one hour! Action is taken to correct the problem immediately. These customers and suppliers work together as one extended family, with trust and a spirit of mutual benefit.

Listen to Your Customer

Quality is defined not by a team's perception of quality, but by the standards and expectations of its customers. Dave, the manager of a local franchise of a national auto repair shop, told our Leadership Development LAB: "An older customer named Helga walked into our shop. Immediately, she complained about 'the guy who used to work here,' and how 'he didn't seem to ever really fix what was wrong with my car.' As she continued explaining her brake repair problems, I listened more intently than I usually do — I used both ears this time. I wrote down the problems as she explained them, keeping good eye contact the whole time, and letting her know by my actions that we were genuinely interested in her problems, especially, in solving them.

"I didn't want to be viewed the same way she viewed 'the other guy,' so I made a conscious effort to really see things from her point of view. As I did it became easier for me to see how natural it was for her to be upset, frustrated, and to feel the shop had let her down.

By the end of the day we'd repaired her car to her liking, and made a very happy customer out of Helga. She will definitely bring her business back to us whenever she needs car repairs because she can tell we take the time to listen to her problems and do the job right. She has learned to trust us through the simple act of listening. Of course she will tell her friends of her experience and recommend us whenever they need their cars repaired. Helga was so pleased that she told us she would come back later in the week with a surprise. The guys in the shop didn't really expect to see Helga back again so soon, but there she was, early Friday morning with a box of three dozen maple bars for us to share. They were really delicious. There is something about a gift that makes it taste much better.

The lesson I learned from this experience is the empowerment that comes to me and others when I practice being a good listener. When I pay attention to my customers and show them I really care, they do respond positively. They always come back to me if I take the time to really care for them.

Empowering leaders lead by example. Dave's example of listening, caring and genuinely seeking to serve, which resulted in Helga's gift, must have made a big impression on all the other team members in Dave's shop. The reward in this case was very tangible. What are you doing to set examples of listening, caring, and genuine interest? The best test, the acid test, is the results you see and the responses you experience. What kind of rewards are you reaping from your examples?

In the past, quality was most often considered reliability, meeting specifications every time. Our understanding of quality is more broad today. There is little point in reliably meeting specifications that are not those desired by the customer. The product may never fail, yet it may be out-of-date technically or perform below the customer's standards. Remember that the customer is the world's greatest expert on quality.

Lasting Impressions

I recently visited the largest, most impressive electronics merchandising sales center I have ever been to. When I walked in, I was a little surprised. A positive, friendly greeter handed me a little chartreuse 2" x 3" slip of paper, which instructed "Please present this form to the most helpful and friendly employee you meet today." The organization referred to their most helpful employees as heroes. As I walked through the spacious store, I was greeted by many friendly, enthusiastic, warm salespeople. It seemed obvious to me that this "hero" idea was working extremely well.

I still had the hero form in my pocket when I got to the check-out stand. There was no waiting. I immediately stepped up to the counter. The check-out person was talking with another employee, which I must admit always bothers me. I feel the customer should be the center of attention and that staff should not be gossiping.

I took out my credit card. The check-out person asked me for picture identification, an unusual request. I took out my driver's license. I was somewhat preoccupied and just a little irritated by the conversation between the two employees. It seemed that she looked at my driver's license.

After a few minutes of having both my driver's license and credit card lying on the counter, I picked up my driver's license and put it back in my billfold. She put my credit card through the machine. Then she returned her attention to me for a moment and said, "I need a picture ID."

My response was, "I showed you a picture ID. You were paying more attention to the other salesperson than you were to me." I reached in my billfold and took out my driver's license again.

It was an awkward moment for all three of us. The other person quietly walked away. The check-out person did her best through casual conversation to make up for the situation and calm what was obviously an irritated customer. She never did apologize, however. My experience is that most people do not know how to apologize. All it takes is a simple, "I apologize," no excuse, no defending. It would have made a world of difference to me.

I relate this experience because all of the positive greetings I had earlier in the store were erased by one disinterested person. This last impression is so important because it capped off my shopping experience. It was the final — and lasting — impression in my memory. I went there to pick up a bargain, and I did. Still, this parting left me with a bad taste in my mouth.

How about your organization? What are you doing to ensure that your customer's final impression will create positive memories?

The best way to start is with what we at Turbo Management Systems call a Customer Value Analysis. Armed with this analysis, top management can work with teams throughout the organization to create an environment in which all associates make changes in their work and work environment to enhance the customer's perception of the value received. This process involves the following six steps:

1.   Identify the team's customers by using the brainstorming process. The focus should be on those customers your team deals with directly on a day-to-day basis.

2.   Identify the products and services that your team provides to each customer. After the team has brainstormed all its internal and external customers, it should define the products and services provided to each of those customers.

3.   **Develop a series of questions to ask each customer.** These should only be used as guidelines for the interview. Team members should not feel compelled to ask only the questions developed by the team, particularly if the customer wants to discuss other areas of team performance. Some performance areas about which your team can inquire include: quality, quantity, timeliness, accuracy, availability, flexibility, and courtesy.

4.   **Decide on a method for obtaining customer feedback.** Conduct a personal interview. This permits the team member to ask follow-up questions and clarify any vague or ambiguous statements. Conduct a telephone interview: this is most appropriate for customers who are frequently out of the office or at another location. The customer may be sent a copy of the questions in advance to facilitate the interview.

Here are some guidelines for conducting customer interviews: Avoid becoming defensive or explaining away negative feedback. This may make the customer defensive and unwilling to continue the interview. Explain to the customer that your team would like to continuously receive feedback on its performance. This is the only way any team can serve its customers well. Keep in mind that any feedback, positive or negative, will help you serve your customers better. However, try to keep the customer focused on "how it should be" rather than "what is wrong."

Ask open-ended questions to draw out your customer. For example, "What would you like to see our team do in order to improve our service to you?" Your goal during the interview should be to obtain as much specific feedback as possible about the team's performance with respect to that customer.

General comments should be followed up by specific questions. If the customer makes general comments such as, "Your team is doing okay" or "I don't really have any complaints," ask specific follow-up questions such as "What could we do to improve quality?"

5. **Analyze customer feedback.** After the team has interviewed all its internal and external customers, the next step is to analyze the *information* in a team meeting. First, determine whether the feedback received relates to the inquiring team's performance. After this decision is made, the team is ready to discuss whether the customer feedback identifies any possible quality or performance measures. Each team member may prepare a brief summary of customer feedback. Each team member should have an opportunity to review all the customer feedback prior to the team meeting. Based on the customer feedback, the team may also have to do some problem-solving to address some immediate customer concerns.

6. **Identify team performance measures.** During a team meeting, the team should brainstorm all of the possible team performance and quality measures that were identified through the customer feedback. For example, the team's customers may have stated that the turnaround time on completion of projects was slow. As a consequence, the team could measure their turnaround time from the time they received the request to the time the project is completed. Similar projects could be compared using this as a measure of the team's performance. Another example would be customer complaints. The team could measure user satisfaction as a performance measure.

Armed with the customer analysis and empowered to make its own decisions, your team will be well on the road to self-management. A self-managing team — one in which members support, encourage and rely upon one another — will make the optimum use of customer feedback. Performance teams feel challenged and motivated to succeed. When teams reach this place or cohesiveness, they need little direction or control from top management. They begin to automatically fly *in formation*.

* Create a culture that willingly gives customers "the shirt off your back."

* Continually improve quality to exceed customer's expectations.

* Recognize that there are internal, as well as external, customers.

* Last impressions make lasting impressions.

* Ask your customers for their feedback.

Basic Elements Of Any Process

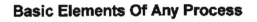

Inputs ⇨   **The Work Process**   ⇨   **Outputs**

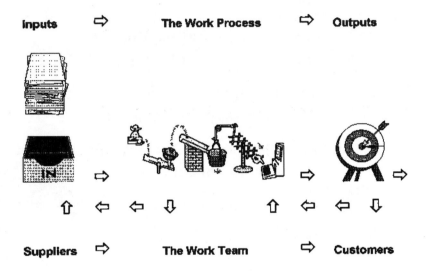

Suppliers ⇨   **The Work Team**   ⇨   **Customers**

7

Productive Processes

In most companies the cost of quality,
including customer complaints,
product liability lawsuits, redoing defective work,
products scrapped, etc.,
runs from 20-40 percent of sales.

Dr. Joseph M. Juran

When Turbo Management Systems began working with the management team of a large furniture retailer several years ago, we started by examining profit drain that resulted from repeat service calls. The problem seemed to stem from the way orders were originally accepted by the finance department and then handed off to the shipping department. I suggested we stop and create a process flow map, starting from the time the sale is made until the customer receives the furniture. The president was impatient with all the time this 'mapping' process was taking. He felt I was asking a lot of dumb questions and everyone should already know the answers. He knew each service call was costing the business a minimum of $75, and that the company was averaging three service calls per sale. Something had to be done. As we began documenting each step in the process, we found many forks in the road, duplicated work and uncertainty about authority, responsibility and policy. "No wonder we have so many problems with complaints and damages," he said. The result of studying and evaluating the company's process was better discipline in accepting sales orders and a more streamlined procedure that ultimately benefited customers.

Study The Process

The furniture retailer saved money by understanding the internal flow of work through the organization. Knowing the answer to the seemingly simple question, "How do we do our work?" is the beginning of managing for continuous improvement. If geese did not make their annual vigil south each year and flew off in different directions, the species would not survive. Getting your team and its processes *in formation* is necessary for survival. After we have clarified our vision, mission and values, have agreed that change is needed, and have defined what our customers want, we can then analyze the process by which work is performed. A process is made up of a series of related work activities leading from a set of inputs that creates state changes and result in outputs that have added value. In other words, it is how we do our work.

People almost always want to do a good job. Problems result when team members have inadequate skills or knowledge. More often, problems stem from the nature of the work process and the way people work together. Often when problems are discovered, the first reaction is to place blame. When something goes wrong, it must be someone's fault. Someone must be made to feel guilty so it will never happen again. Right? Wrong!

The process cannot be improved by blaming, punishing, or rewarding. The process can only be improved by studying, analyzing, modifying and studying further.

Blaming creates fear, which reduces improvement efforts. Studying the process creates knowledge, a true learning organization, and knowledge is required for meaningful improvement efforts. Studying to improve the process is one of the fundamental purposes of the performance team. An effective process adds maximum value at minimum cost for the customer. A sloppy process often evolves over time through tradition, rather than through thoughtful analysis. Quality suffers.

To fully understand all the steps in a process, let's start with something simple, say, baking a birthday cake. If you are planning to bake a cake, one micro-process may be as simple as blending the ingredients. Another micro-process would be actually baking the cake in the oven for a period of time.

Process improvement is a technique of improving quality while reducing costs by eliminating waste in small bites. It focuses attention on each of the steps from the initial client contact, all the way through to the clients' successful use. If every step is efficient and effective, waste and costs will be reduced. Each roadblock we encounter, each step that requires extra effort, wastes time and money, even when you are baking a cake. Wasted steps in this cake baking process are shown with an asterisk.

MACRO PROCESSES
1. Mix ingredients
2. Bake cake in oven
3. Frost cake

MINI PROCESSES
1. Buy cake mix
2. Buy all other ingredients needed
3. Blend ingredients in bowl
4. Pour blended ingredients in cake pan
5. Put cake pan in oven
6. Bake prescribed length of time
7. Remove cake from oven
8. Frost the cake
9. Add candles

MICRO PROCESSES
1. Check cupboard for cake mix
      * Go to the store and buy cake mix
2. Check recipe for ingredients
      * Buy milk, eggs, etc.
3. Open box of cake mix
4. Get mixing bowl from cupboard
5. Empty cake mix into bowl
6. Add other ingredients
7. Position mixer to mix ingredients
      * Not washed from earlier — wash mixer
8. Beat ingredients until mixed
9. Pour ingredients in cake pan
      * Cake pan not greased — stop and grease pan lightly
10. Put cake in oven
      * Oven needs to be pre-heated first — wait until ready
11. Bake cake prescribed time
12. Check to see if the cake is finished

* Timer broken, have to check watch, not effective
   timer
13. Return to oven for a few minutes until finished
14. Remove cake from oven
    * Forgot hot pads, close oven door and find pads
15. Remove cake from pan
16. Cool cake for a few hours
17. Get frosting mix
    * Don't have right flavor — back to store
18. Get spatula
19. Frost cake
20. Count out correct number of candles
21. Put candles on cake.

A MACRO PROCESS in your organization could be, for example, selling the job. The MINI-PROCESS could be getting a sales lead, making an appointment, seeing the client or closing the sale. Finally, the MICRO-PROCESS can be drawn as the receptionist takes a phone call and passes the lead to the sales department. The salesperson calls to get an appointment, learns of prospect's requirements, makes a presentation, follows up on prospect, answers questions and sells the job. Plot your actual steps, every one of them, to understand which processes need to be changed and which need to be left alone. The performance team focuses on preventing problems before they occur instead of finding and fixing problems or defects after the fact.

Proper Process Empowers

I had just begun working with a large glass manufacturer. While setting up the conference room before a team training session, I stumbled upon a huge 'sign' in the closet.

On closer inspection, I saw that the sign was actually a process flow map, almost 10 feet long by five feet high, detailing every step in the macro-process from the time glass arrived from the supplier at the receiving dock until the finished tempered lites left their shipping dock. The organization had paid a consultant over $30,000 to analyze the firm's processes and create the process flow map.

There was only one problem. The people who needed to understand the processes intimately didn't. The only person who fully understood the organization's macro process was the consultant. So there's $30,000 down the drain, or in this case, stuffed away in a closet.

We began working with the top 29 people in the organization on how to analyze their process within each performance area. We taught the following fundamentals:

* All work flows through a process.
* Most processes don't happen by intent, but evolve over time.
* All processes can be improved.
* The more steps in a process, the more opportunity for failure.
* Errors hide in a sloppy process.

After a few weeks, Rob, the superintendent of the tinted window line, reported back to class. Standing there in his bib overalls and chewing a wad of tobacco, Rob showed us the process he and his team had documented. It took over 47 steps to cut, bevel and bug the glass on his special product line.

"Now," Rob said, never letting up on his chew, "That is one sloppy process."

Rob went on to say that by analyzing the process, the team found they could eliminate 12 steps. The process was reduced from 59 steps to 47 steps, and that was just the beginning. They ultimately reduced the process to 29 steps.

Remaining competitive requires that we re-think work from the ground up, cutting out any unnecessary steps in the process. It's far more important to ensure effectiveness than to honor time-bound traditions. Those who participate in the process must be empowered to change it.

Steps To Improve Your Process

1. Define output requirements.

When you developed your customers' requirements, you defined what you do that adds value. By transforming inputs to outputs, something of greater value is created. How is your product or service used that makes it of value? This important question defines the purpose of your process. You cannot successfully follow and improve a process without knowing what you want that process to accomplish.

2. Define input requirements.

Quality problems can occur by not specifying the requirements for the input. Too often we hear team members say, "We have a problem with input, but purchasing controls that!" For whom does purchasing purchase? Purchasing is a supplier to manufacturing. Buying based on price alone can increase costs by creating production problems.

Taking a fresh perspective helped reduce costs for a Midwestern landscape contractor. The company had a very large holding yard for plant material. The chief officer thought that it made sense to buy truckload after truckload of plant material each spring, put it into the holding yard and maintain it. Thus, the plants would be ready for use whenever a job called for them. By analyzing the processes, the team determined that maintaining stock for long periods was extraordinarily expensive. The owner went back to suppliers and said, "Look, it's not our job to hold all this material! We'll continue to buy from you, but you keep it in stock in your yard until we're ready for it." He said his company did not mind paying a little extra for the plant material as long as the plants were on the job when needed. They were not in the nursery business; they were landscape contractors. They got rid of their contract yard and saved themselves grief, aggravation and expense.

The team must contribute to defining the requirements for its input. You cannot be held accountable for quality, costs and speed if you are suffering under a system that provides input but does not meet your requirements.

3. Define the value-adding state changes.

Activities, or work steps, revolve around state changes. The key steps in a process reflect state changes, which occur when the product changes form, or transforms. Every state change is intended to add value. Your work process is a transformational process. For example, the accounting process transforms incoming numbers into reformatted numbers and reports that provide added value. The numbers must change state if they are to be of greater value.

Each of these state changes can be measured statistically. States may change with little or great variability. The stability of your process can best be seen at the point of state changes. Knowing your state changes and developing measures (discussed in the next chapter) are critical to managing a process for quality.

4. Place current activity steps on a flow-chart.

A flow-chart illustrates in sequential order what we do to create transformation. The performance team writes down all its activities on 4" x 6" colored post-it notes, then sticks the notes on the wall in order of normal occurrence. This is an easy way to develop a flow-chart of your process that your team can readily visualize. Now analyzing the process will become much easier.

When making your flow chart, it is helpful to use symbols and colors to identify different types of activities. Here are some common symbols. Your team may develop tailored symbols for your specific activities.

◆	(Purple)	Decisions
■	(Green)	Work Activities or Operations
●	(Red)	Delays
▲	(Yellow)	Inspection
⇨	(Blue)	Transport/Move

5. Analyze variances and brainstorm solutions.

A variance is the gap between the status quo and error free performance, a deviation from standards. Any quality problem is a variance, and any variance is an opportunity for improvement. A distribution center ships electrical components to branches, but once in a while, a wrong part is shipped. This is a variance from specifications or standard performance. What is it about the process of work that causes the variance?

6. Analyze cycle times and eliminate waste.

In the old days, efficiency experts sought to make workers more productive. They did 'time-and-motion studies' to determine 'standards' that were then imposed on workers. This system assumed a static work process. The focus was not on improving the work process, but on controlling the workers. Changing the process just confused the standards, requiring another time-and-motion study to develop an up-to-date standard.

This system is dead! What has proved most successful is to give the performance teams the responsibility for continually improving their process. Quality and productivity improve simultaneously when the team focuses on eliminating waste. Therefore, standards are not needed. When team members can directly improve their work process to better serve their customer, they are not merely involved, they are empowered.

7. Reduce cycle time.

Cycle time is the space between input and output of materials, *information* or other resources used in the process. Increasing speed has nothing to do with workers working harder and faster! Eliminating waste and improving the speed of the work process are corollary. In other words, when you eliminate waste, you increase speed. To increase speed, you must eliminate waste. There are many different kinds of waste that occur in a work process:

Wasted effort.
Rework, restudy, re-plan, reconsider, review, repair.
Wasted space.
Wasted product in inventory.
Wasted product in process.
Wasted product defects.
Wasted transportation.

As we often examine the steps in an operation, we find that as the material flows through the process, it spends more time waiting than in actual production. Most of this waiting is waste, which impacts quality! An interruption-free, continuous process eliminates delay. Materials As Needed (MAN) inventory systems are based on creating an interruption-free flow, both within production sites, and between production sites. Speed of operations increases as delays are removed.

Speed is not only an issue in the factory. How long does it take your organization to make a decision on capital expenditures? How long does it take to hire a new team member? How long does it take to get a piece of equipment repaired? How long does it take to change a process that does not work well? How long does it take to develop a new computer program?

You can reduce cycle time by evaluating the process. If you've got a particularly vexing procedure in your company that is eating up too many worker hours and too much money, try breaking down the process in the following way:

1. Total number of time units (minutes, hours, days)? _____
2. Total number of current process steps? _____
3. Target process cycle time? _____
4. Which steps can be eliminated? _____
5. Which steps can be combined? _____
6. Which steps can be completed faster? _____
7. Which steps can be simplified? _____
8. Which steps can be rearranged? _____

Armed with this *information*, you can now develop an ideal process flow. Following procedures without a focus on wowing the customer cannot provide the continuous improvement you need to succeed. A process stream is a means of tracking whether a job or process is on target and will produce a product or service of high caliber.

One eddy at Tube Forgings of America was the die stamp set-up time. The die set up is a micro-process in the macro-process of stamping pipe tubes, elbows and couplings. By studying this micro-process, the tube forgings team was able to reduce some of the set-up time from four hours, a norm that had been accepted for years, to 45 minutes.

The philosophy of incremental improvement means looking at obstacles, one by one, and determining how to remove them. Make each improvement more customer-focused. Measure how each of the changes you make in the processes along the line affect the end product and your customer. Consider our example of baking a cake. This seemingly simple task — even when you use a store-bought mix — can still be rife with barriers that prevent you from presenting a beautifully decorated confection at Grandpa's birthday party. Consider all the delays shown in our example. Many of them could have been removed had our baker simply looked ahead to project potential problems.

EEEEEE

I taught a class at a steel distribution center that cuts steel plates to customer specifications using an automatic computer-controlled burner plate. As we began talking about inefficient processes, Bill, the plant manager, interrupted me and asked, "So you want to see an example of a really sloppy process?"

At the break, he led me out to where a 20-foot x 30-foot plate of steel was being cut into six capital "E" pieces.

The pieces were laid out end to end, cookie-cutter style — EEEEEE. He looked at me, and I looked at him. The problem was obvious. Each plate created as much scrap as finished product. Had the programmer in the office positioned the pieces jigsaw-style, rather than end to end, the organization could have realized a 30 percent greater yield per steel plate.

The operator was only held accountable for how many parts he cut per day. He was not accountable for maximum yield. Had he spoken up, it would have only slowed down his own process. In fact, all it would have led to was personal grief. There was no incentive for him to speak up.

Process Development Comes in Many Colors

At Zidell, a barge manufacturer, workers consistently complained they could never find the right rigging for the job. After a short brainstorming session, someone came up with the idea of color-coding the rigging to the hanging brackets. They began color-coding all the cables, straps and chains with the storage hooks on which they belonged. It was now far easier to locate and return the proper equipment to its rightful place. This *information* created a definite process improvement.

At another of our process-improvement meetings, everyone agreed, "We don't have enough 220 outlets."

"How many do you have?" I asked.

"Not enough," was the reply.

No one seemed to know how many 220 outlets there were or where they were located. The maintenance manager drew up a floor plan showing the outlet locations, shared it with the team and color-coded the 220 and 110 outlets with contrasting fluorescent paint. This is *information*!

Zidell has improved many processes in a short period of time, including the way it orders parts, stages materials and communicates between engineering and production (which has resulted in better, more accurate as-built drawings). The president congratulated the Zidell team after a customer commented to him: "This barge is twice as good as the last barge you built for us."

The president then added that he had recently attended the delivery and launching of a competitor's barge and overheard the same customer say, "You know, this barge is twice as good as your last one."

We can never rest on our laurels. Once geese have flown south for the winter, they don't spend their days basking in the sun. They know, instinctively, that they will return north on an arduous journey to procreate their species. We celebrate each achieved goal and then move on to even greater excellence.

* **All work flows through a process.**

* **Performance teams study and improve their processes.**

* **Waste hides in a sloppy process.**

* **Analyze processes to eliminate quality variances.**

* **Strive to continually improve your process.**

Strive for Perfection — OR ELSE! [1]

If 99.9 percent is good enough, then...
- Two million documents will be lost by the IRS this year.
- 811,000 faulty rolls of 35 mm film will be loaded this year.
- 22,000 checks will be deducted from the wrong bank accounts in the next 60 minutes.
- 1,314 phone calls will be misplaced by telecommunication services every minute.
- 12 babies will be given to the wrong parents each day.
- 268,500 defective tires will be shipped this year.
- 14,208 defective personal computers will be shipped this year.
- 103,260 income tax returns will be processed incorrectly this year.
- 2 plane landings daily at Chicago's O'Hare Airport will be unsafe.
- 3,056 copies of tomorrow's Wall Street Journal will be missing one of the three sections.
- 18,322 pieces of mail will be mishandled in the next hour.
- 291 pacemaker operations will be performed incorrectly this year.
-114,500 mismatched pairs of shoes will be shipped this year.
- 107 incorrect medical procedures will be performed by the end of today.
- 315 entries in Webster's Third New International Dictionary of the English Language will turn out to be misspelled.

---

[1] *insight,* Syncrude Canada Ltd., Communications Division

8

Meaningful Measures

Of course, perfection is impossible, but...it is always possible for one organization to be better than another, and for improvement to be continuous and unlimited...
Quality, therefore, is a dynamic process, which enables the good to survive.

David Hutchin
Quality Circles Handbook

Will, the owner of eight auto repair centers, told our Leadership Development LAB: "During the last half of 1993, Darrin, a technician in one of our shops, only managed to accomplish about average production rates. The truth is, his production dramatically fluctuated from month to month. Some months he was really up, other months really down, with far too many down months. I happened to hear that Darrin was looking for another job. I was surprised at the end of the year to learn that Darrin turned out to be the number-one producer out of 32 technicians in eight shops! It was his personal best month, a 'world's record' for him. December traditionally is our slowest month, so this was really a big achievement.

As soon as I finished compiling the data, I couldn't wait to tell him the great news. I called him and said, 'Darrin, let me be the first to congratulate you on being the number - one producer in our entire company for the month of December, and, for setting a new 'personal-best.' Darrin was really surprised. He didn't have any idea that he'd just had his best month ever - he just knew he'd been working hard, and had been very busy.

Darrin was so happy that I'd called to congratulate him that he told me his goal was to win the title of technician of the year. Then in January he was number one again, and set yet another 'world's record' for his own performance. This time I talked to his manager about it and together we decided to give him a raise. By this time he was pumped. He went on to be our technician of the year. Darrin still has his mood swings, I guess we all do, but his downs aren't so low anymore, and they don't last as long. His highs are higher and last longer.

The lesson I learned from this experience is the importance of keeping score and the power of truly recognizing and rewarding good performance. Darrin is now more committed to his personal goals.

The action I call you to is to look for the things in your team members' performance that can be scored and recorded. When you see performance improvements, jump all over it, dramatize the achievements. Use scorekeeping as the basis for formally recognizing, and reward meaningful performance improvement. The benefit you will gain is only improved productivity, and a more dedicated team."

Meaningful measurement is *information* for the performance team about its level of performance. A meaningful measurement system, a scorekeeping system, is an ongoing mechanism for providing *information* in a timely meaningful manner.

Has any team ever performed at its best with no knowledge of its performance, no feedback, no scoreboard? It is unlikely. In athletics, there is a passion for numbers, an intense desire to know how well we are doing. Golfers carry a scorecard in their back pocket, mark down their score at each hole, compare it to their previous score on that same hole, and compute whether they are currently ahead or behind their previous performance on this course. It is the fun and challenge of the game.

Runners who maintain their efforts keep score. They may even keep a log, a graph or chart on the number of miles per week, minutes per mile, cumulative miles per year. Their goal - break last year's record; set a new record for miles in a month; set a new record for quickest time over this three-mile stretch. And all of this scorekeeping has nothing to do with anyone else. It has nothing to do with applause from the stands. It is entirely for the purpose of self-management.

Learning Organization

Competitive pressures brought on the quality revolution that began in the early '80's. Most major U.S. corporations have implemented varied forms of statistical process controls. Clearly a new emphasis on measurements arose. Still, relatively few organizations have actually initiated measurement-based systems, and even fewer are measuring the right things! Many use measures negatively to downsize, cut costs, or control and evaluate personnel. Values-based organizations use measures to reward, recognize, empower, gain competitive advantage, create jobs, increase effectiveness, improve service and win. They use measurement as the source of information for creating a learning organization, a smart organization where every team member learns every day from the feedback of their work processes. The performance team learns how and where to change and improve its processes for continuous improvement.

If you do not have a learning organization, you rely on people in a few positions of authority and power to come up with all the improvements. In a learning organization, all team members are learning how to do their work better, easier, faster, safer, with greater excellence.

Measurement

The starting point for a learning organization is an understanding of our current levels of performance. This is where measurement comes in. Measurement means we aren't performing based on how we feel or think about things, what I call 'management by superstition,' instead, there is an exacting comparison to past performance. Team members may disagree over unsubstantiated opinions about problems and their causes; these disputes can lead to unproductive conflict and poor decision making. In a learning organization, all team members know specifically what percentage of their work efforts are producing intended results, scrap and rework. Because of this we can determine specifically how long it takes to create 'value-added' state changes, which create 'value-added' output.

The language of measurement is statistics, a tool for handling data. Statistical measures provide evidence for making decisions about a process. Statistics don't fix problems, but they can highlight problems and their common causes so that the team responsible for the process can make needed corrections.

Variation statistics function on the fact that every process exhibits some degree of variation. The measurement of that variation and the understanding of the sources of that variation make statistics an extremely valuable tool. There are two kinds of variation: random with common causes and non-random with special causes. Common cause variation is inherent in a process. This type of variation is 'normal' to a process and will not go away unless the process is changed drastically. Special cause variation is not inherent in a process. This kind of variation is not normal to the process and often causes a process to be out of control.

A variance is different than variability. A variance is something beyond the system's normal performance. There are two kinds of variances. One is variance from normal system performance, which was just described. The other is variance from customer requirements. You may produce a computer program that works perfectly. The only problem is there may be other similar programs performing twice as many functions at the same price. Competitors create higher customer expectations and you lose customers. Your product now 'varies' from customer requirements. This is a quality problem, not a defect. Your product is not perceived by the customer to be a 'quality' product because it is inferior in function. This is a variance and must be corrected if you are to remain in business. The second way to improve the system is to raise the mean, the normative standard of performance.

This is often called a breakthrough. In both cases, it will be helpful to have information that lets you know what is normal for the system.

To avoid the problem of a special cause variance/random and continually show improvement, the team needs to have the skills to quantify work processes and to gather and analyze information systematically. The greatest opportunities for improvement must be identified, root causes determined, alternative courses of action evaluate, and meaningful measurements put into place in order to maintain gains. This cycle of events demands the use of reliable methods for gathering, representing and analyzing information. Performance teams must understand how to use measurement methods from simple checklists and histograms (a kind of bar chart) to specially designed experiments.

System Performance

Every system, whether it is a pizza parlor, an airline, or a sales organization, produces a pattern of data. The team must understand this pattern. For instance, a pizza parlor may average 100 pepperoni pizzas a day, but it will be a rare day on which the restaurant sells exactly 100. And, it will be almost impossible for the restaurant to sell 100 units every day. One day it may sell 105, the next 97, the next 102, the next 93, and so forth. It averages 100. This pattern within the system is a normal distribution, or normal variability. This variability forms a pattern, with approximately half of the days falling below the mean of 100, and about half above, with the greatest number of days falling close to 100.

The causes of variation within this system we call 'common cause.' In other words, if the manager asks, "But how come today the sales team sold only 92 units?" The only sensible answer is that nothing is wrong; this is normal variability within the system. It is simply random performance. If everything is held constant, and there are no changes or anything unusual influencing performance, you will see this amount of variation. It is also true that when the performance is at 105, there is nothing especially good happening either. This, too, is random performance within the system.

It is useful to compare performance in units of time (hours, days, weeks or months) on an ongoing basis, to see the comparison to the normal distribution. This is the essence of statistical process control. Knowing the normative statistics, the distribution, you can define upper and lower control limits. For example, if the restaurant only sells 50 pepperoni pizzas when the pattern generally falls between 90 and 110, for example, it is clear that this performance indicates that something outside of the system has occurred. There is a variance, a special cause. Something has happened abnormal from the performance of the system. Now it will make sense to problem-solve the source of this 'special cause' variance. Why has this happened? It cannot be explained by the normal system. It is outside of the system.

Benchmarking

Traditionally, we define benchmarking as a progress check. We compare ourselves to the leading organization in our field and see how we measure up and we attempt to emulate their success. When many people think customer service, Nordstrom automatically comes to mind. Even if you are not in the clothing business, you can still learn from their example. For instance, do you accept returns with a smile?

Identify and study the best. Ask yourself, who is the leader in environmental management? Consider Ben & Jerry's. What about training? Many people look to Polaroid or General Electric as setting the standards. When benchmarking, you need not limit yourself to large, national corporations or chains. There may be an outstanding example of innovative marketing or service right in your back yard. Powell's Books here in Portland, Oregon, dramatically reduced turnover and greatly boosted morale by paying a large portion of each team member's child care costs.

Strategic benchmarking is picking the areas of your business that you wish to be superior in, because you have determined by being superior in that area you can gain a strategic advantage. After you have determined the area(s) where you wish to have a strategic advantage, you benchmark with the best in that area of performance, whether inside or outside of your industry.

Areas for benchmarking could be in billing cycle time, inventory turns, maximum utilization of space, customer service, redesign and creation of new products, research and development, and generating new ideas for new products.

Benchmark today to judge effectiveness of future changes:
1. Timeliness of responses to requests—internal and external.
2. Cost of each deliverable—internal and external.
3. Customer satisfaction—internal and external.
4. Culture as perceived by all team members.
Then...
5. Establish goals for each performance measure.
6. Integrate the strategies used by others.
7. Become a benchmark for others to follow.

Performance Criteria Data

In the past, measurements were taken by middle management and reported to upper management. Charts displaying sales, profits and annual performance (results criteria data) were used on an 'after the fact' basis at quarterly and year-end meetings. These measurements did not get to the root of problems. This would be like an NBA team measuring wins of the season with no regard to free throw percentages.

Just as basketball teams have statistics for almost everything - rebound percentages, turnovers, assists, percentages of free throws, steals, percentages of shots from behind the three-point line- an *in formation* organization doesn't merely measure results (baskets) at the end of the process. An *in formation* organization measures performance within the process. The team must choose carefully which and how many performance indicators to measure.

Performance teams measure what is important to their customers, such as response times, quality of work, failure rate, etc. They display the results of their measurements on trend charts and bar graphs. These are the tools (scoreboard) utilized to keep every one on the team *informed* about the goals and their current level of performance.

If you were building engines, there are performance measures to indicate how well the engine should run once it is completely assembled. When the piston rings are placed around the pistons, the tightness can be measured. When the pistons are placed within the cylinder block, the resistance when they move up and down the cylinder can be measured. Virtually every step in the process can be measured to determine whether or not the process is in control, and feedback immediately can be provided to the worker.

The performance team needs to brainstorm all possible measures and agree on the quality measures most critical in order to provide superior customer service.

Feedback

Soon after graduating from high school I bought a 1952 Chevrolet convertible. The body was customized and it was powered by a '55 Chevrolet V-8 engine and transmission. Unfortunately the speedometer cable wouldn't connect to the transmission. I moved to Cleveland, Ohio, and made the commute home to Ann Arbor, Michigan, many weekends over the next couple of years. On those long drives home, though I tried to follow traffic, I know I yielded to the temptation to push it many times. Everything would be okay until a policeman started to follow me and then I would break out in a cold sweat. That was when I realized first hand the fear, frustration and anxiety which can be caused when you "don't know the score" and someone in control has all the pertinent information. I needed that feedback from my speedometer in order to feel in control as I tackled the road ahead.

It is essential that every performance team have full knowledge of their performance, they must establish a measurement system that provides timely and useful performance feedback.

There are many misconceptions about feedback. Some of them are just excuses for not taking the time and effort required. Some are genuine fears and misunderstandings.

In the bakery line of a cookie plant at Nabisco, a key objective was controlling the amount of broken product. The performance team posted graphs showing the cost of broken cookies produced on each line on a daily and weekly basis. Each graph had a colored band showing a target level of scrap costs and a line showing actual performance. Daily highlights of scrap performance for each line were written on a flipchart by the team Subject Area Expert. Once this feedback became visible to the team, the department met its scrap goal for the first time in years.

Results-to-resources ratios provide a particularly useful kind of feedback. Hits divided by at-bats, golf strokes versus par, completed passes divided by attempts, % of free throws, % of 3 pointers, % of turnovers, finished parts punched per foot of metal plates purchased are all forms of this kind of feedback. It enables you to celebrate each improvement, while balancing customers' needs with your team's own needs.

Performance teams must understand the results-to-resources ratio concept and accept that their responsibility as a performance team is to know, track, and continually show improvement in these results. It's easy to understand when thinking of a restaurant. For instance, a waiter's results might be the number of desserts sold with each meal. The resources are the number of customers. If she sells 20 desserts to 30 customers, she's got a 2-to-3 results-to-resource ratio, or about 66 percent. If you know your ratio, that establishes a target for you to exceed.

Achieving increasingly higher % is how teams score with their customers and the owners. The results measured should be limited to those over which the team has control. Consider some results you might want to measure: Quality Achieved; Profit or Return; Cost; Throughput; Timeliness; Changes Implemented; Sales/Closes; Accuracy; Deliveries Completed; Goals Attained; Production; Customers Served.

It is the team's responsibility now to list major resources or opportunities available to produce these intended results. These are measurable elements from categories such as time periods, facility, space, people, equipment, materials and money. The team then considers the resources at their disposal: Tools; Space Committed; Assets; Expenses; People; Hours; Wages; Occurrences; Submission; Inputs of any Type; Projects Completed; Tries/attempts; Contracts.

Now the intended results need to be matched to the resources available/selected and ranked in order of importance.

Measuring And Chartering Suppliers

Steve, the distribution center manager for a large bakery, told our Leadership Development LAB: "Our department had submitted several work repair orders to our maintenance department for much-needed equipment repairs in the distribution center. The response time on these repair orders, in my opinion, would make a snail seem fast. The elapsed time between the requests and the repairs was steadily declining. As a result, our shipping department people had, in many cases, started making the needed repairs themselves. Morale in my department was low. We needed to feel that we were part of a real team with the full support of the maintenance department. We needed their full cooperation if we were going to ship on schedule, keep our labor costs in line, and meet our customers' deadlines. We needed to be treated like valued customers and experience the same kind of service responsiveness we all expect in a fast food restaurant, bank or retail store.

Along with everyone else in the department, I was guilty of grumbling and complaining. Of course that just made things worse. I wanted to move out of the complain, blame, and shame mode. To do this, I knew we needed to problem solve. An important part of real problem solving is the gathering of relevant data. In this case, we needed hard data on response times. So I started a notebook listing all submitted work orders, along with the nature of the repair needed. I listed the dates and times the requests were submitted. I began touring the shipping area on a daily basis, checking on the status of the maintenance work that had been requested. Then I posted and circulated a chart showing average maintenance department response times per day, week and month.

These efforts have resulted in repairs being completed in a far more timely manner, making my job much easier. Morale in our department is up. Our team feels like valued customers who can count on quick, courteous, competent repair service.

The lesson I learned from this experience is that if I am enthusiastic and move away from complaining, blaming and shaming to problem solving, including the collection and charting of relevant data, my enthusiasm carries over to others and jobs get completed with much more agreeable response times.

The action I call you to is be enthusiastic in whatever you are doing. Don't complain, blame or shame; get the facts, the real facts, and keep everyone informed of both positive and negative trends. Based on my experience, I can guarantee that your positive approach will carry over to your co-workers and suppliers.

The benefit you will gain is the completion of your projects more quickly, lowered costs, and happy customers. Every person's job will be easier, and this will add meaning and purpose for everyone on the team."

Measure For Measure

* When you bring your performance up to meet your goals, that is called accomplishment. When you bring your goals down to meet your performance, that is called rationalization.
* In the absence of clearly defined goals, we are forced to concentrate on activity and ultimately become enslaved by it.
* Meaningful measurement and benchmarking must precede goal-setting if we want to get buy-in from the team.
* We must challenge and grow the goals on the team, instead of trying to impose them.

High performance teams keep score. What gets measured gets done. If you don't measure a task or performance, you have no way to improve. Improvement derived from baseline measurements inspires motivation. When the team measures performance and sees evidence of meaningful improvement, beating its former best, pride is instilled.

I met with Larry Cartwright, an old friend who is general manager of the Freightliner truck assembly plant. Freightliner, because of its quality reputation, has grown from 12,000 units per year and a 9% market share to 77,000 units per year and a 30% market share. They have more than tripled their work force in 15 years and today employ over 2,000 in three locations in the Portland area. The person hours per truck built have gone from 360 to 120 hours of assembly time. The trucks are custom engineered for each customer. The number of supervisors has gone from one per six or seven people to supervision of one per approximately 100.

Freightliner made these improvements by carefully setting goals and taking measures as those goals came to fruition. The company had a clear destination in mind. Larry told me he had found that the more supervisors he had on the floor, the more problems the organization had. How is this possible? Who lines out the work? The answer - the work is lined out on the computer. There are 200 computer screens in the assembly plant and the employees are trained, and I emphasize trained. They know exactly what to do. They know exactly what the performance standards are; what quality is and what it looks like on their job; and they know what units of production they are accountable for every day.

Larry tells his team members they can do their job in six hours and take coffee breaks the rest of the day as far as he is concerned, as long as they don't disrupt or interfere with the work of other people.

Most of the people in the plant are working at 120% of goal. Larry says, contrary to the opinion of many, that you should continue to raise the mark if you want people to perform at higher levels. He discovered that his team performs at a higher level and become motivated by exceeding the mark. Exceeding the mark stimulates them to consistently higher performance.

When the team is given meaningful *information*, the members will act to improve costs, just as they will act to improve quality. Performance teams usually become more cost-conscious and more conservative than managers, when they are given this responsibility. This usually requires a change in the system for sharing *information*.

Providing the team with meaningful measurement skills isn't enough to ensure their use. Again, the key is to make these methods part of an overall infrastructure that encourages continuous improvement and meaningful involvement. So, while quantitative methods alone cannot be a complete solution, they are an essential part of a successful quality improvement strategy.

* **The teams keep score.**

* **Set measurements, aiming for error-free work.**

* **What gets measured, gets done.**

* **Benchmark your organization with industries outside your own.**

* **Aim for the best.**

Target

I can hit IT!
Can you?
Hit what, you ask?
Hit IT, of course.
Don't ask.
If I knew, I could hit IT.
Where to go, what to pursue.
How about you?
Are you clear on where to go, what to say? How to grow?
What to do, what to pursue?
Okay, I've got it.
I am supposed to get it in my mitt.
Catch it with skill
Not just stand here
Move around with frill
Okay I'll do it.
Oh, just one thing I need to ask
What am I to do, what is the task?

-Larry W. Dennis, Sr.

Determining the Destination

Managers do things right. Leaders do the right thing.
Warren Bennis

Dewey, a supervisor of delivery systems at a dental equipment manufacturing company, told our Leadership Development LAB: "It was the fall of 1994, around the time we usually start our United Way campaigns. I was working in the machine shop when I was approached by two women from the assembly department. They asked if I would like to participate in a creative fundraising activity to increase participation for United Way donations. The fund-raiser consisted of the supervisors and unit specialists allowing their picture to be put on jars and set out in the lunchrooms for employees to fill with money. The one whose jar had the most money at the end of three weeks would have to kiss a pig. I told the women, 'Well, there isn't much risk there. Sure, sign me up. There's no way I'm going to have to kiss a pig!'

The people in my department had a different idea. They had bake sales, rummage sales and garage sales, and the proceeds went into my jar. I have never seen so many people contribute so much money out of their own pockets. Everyone was very generous.

By the end of the three weeks, contributions exceeded $1,450 to my jar. Needless to say, I had to kiss the pig. I am not sure who squirmed the most as I did the deed, the little pig or me! As I was standing up in front of the whole company of over 500 people, I was overwhelmed with such a feeling of pride to represent the people of my department. It wasn't my success, it was theirs.

I have a picture of me with that fat little pig with the red ribbon around it's neck hanging on my office wall. Every time I look at it, I am reminded of how much a great bunch of people can do when they put their hearts and heads together with determination to reach a shared goal.

The action I call you to is to give your team a clear vision of the common goal. Encourage everyone to participate and make it fun. Some may contribute more, some may contribute less, but let everyone share in the feeling of success. The benefit you will gain is a team that is eager to conquer the next challenge that comes along."

Dewey's co-workers set their goal to raise money then set about finding a unique and colorful way to accomplish that goal. The destination in this case was very clearly spelled out in such a way that everyone couldn't help but want to participate. They were motivated by a desire to see Dewey kiss that pig. In the process of working toward their goal, it is likely that morale was boosted as well. And ultimately, they were rewarded in obtaining their financial objective while having fun! Talk about a silk purse from a sow's ear!

Setting Goals

Here is a question for you to consider: Would you be willing to kiss a pig if it meant your team could reach its destination? Dramatizing ideas and putting fun and play into work makes any goal more achievable. What can you do today to break up the routine? Create stories and excitement and thus enliven your team!

You don't have to kiss a pig to get where you want to go, but you and your team need to have a clearly defined set of goals and a plan laid out for achieving them. Setting and measuring goals helps define new heights of excellence and puts the team *in formation*, because you know where you are headed, and you can celebrate each step of the journey together. Geese may not say to themselves, "Hooray, we've crossed North Carolina; only a few more days of flapping and we hit the jackpot in Florida." Still, you know they have to cheer up when they start feeling that sunshine on their wings and know the end is in sight.

During the second afternoon of a two-day Management Team Advance program, Tevis, the president of an organization that manufactures cab protectors for over highway trucks, stared off in the distance and said, "Ah-hah!"

I looked at him. "Tevis, what happened? What's going on?"

He responded, "I just saw it."

I followed his gaze and saw nothing but a blank wall. "Saw what?" I asked, more puzzled than ever.

He smiled, "Five million dollars. Five million dollars in sales."

In that moment, Tevis had set a goal. His organization would aim for $5 million in annual sales, nearly twice its current output.

Everything is created twice, once in the mind and the second time in kind. In his mind, he captured a vision of this stretching goal. Setting this goal energized the team to fly *in formation* and set in motion the purchase of another plant in Denver and the expansion of an existing plant in Memphis. By the end of the third year in which we had worked with this organization, the goal of $5 million in sales had been achieved.

To accomplish a goal, it is important to have a plan. Some goals look good but do not provide the performance team a starting point. Merely writing down a goal, such as "We need to increase productivity," will not accomplish the goal. You need to be specific. "We need to increase productivity by 25 percent, and we will do this by...." is a more concrete goal. Further, everyone on the team must commit to attaining the goal. Engaging the performance team in the goal-setting process makes sense. Strong goals are clear, challenging, measurable, specific and controllable by the performance team.

Establish a pattern of action to support the goal, otherwise, you will render your objective obsolete before the journey even begins. By following a goal-setting process, we can ensure that our goals stand the best possible chance at success. Here are six steps to setting empowering goals:

1. Determine what actually needs to be done.

This may sound simple, but many goals are written based on what happened instead of what really needs to happen. You can find out what is critical by first of all talking to your customers, other performance team members, the area supervisor, a skilled trade's person, or someone in management who is working with your performance team. When you set goals, make sure you have the resources and the ability to complete the project.

A definitive goal statement would be: Always deliver to our customers the right product or service on time at the lowest cost. This broad company statement, really the only goal that counts, creates a list of attainable goals:

* On time delivery must be 90 percent by the end of the year.
* Reduce second-quality products to five percent of production by next season.
* Eliminate all customer claims for incorrect deliveries within five years.

2. Set empowering goals.

When goals are set too high, team members grow frustrated because they never quite attain success. They usually give up. Having zero customer complaints is likely to be an unrealistically high goal. When a goal is set too low, the team completes the goal but gets no satisfaction out of doing so. A goal easily accomplished in the past poses no challenge. A goal that is challenging, yet attainable, brings satisfaction and inspires the team to forge ahead. We only commit to goals we identify with, and we only identify with goals we believe are possible. Measure current levels of performance to establish a base-line.

3. Develop the goals with the team members input.

The performance team sets its own stretching goals based on current levels of performance. It may help to ask internal customers what they feel needs to happen in order for higher performance to be achieved.

4. Prioritize goals.

It is important to determine which goals should be accomplished first. When the performance team is starting out, as in the forming and storming stages, it is best to set goals that can be easily achieved. This builds the performance team's confidence. As the performance team moves into the norming and performing stages, they should set more challenging, tougher goals.

5. Assign action plans for each goal.

Even clearly stated goals may be tough to tackle without a series of action steps describing how the goal is to be accomplished and who is responsible for each step. Writing action steps makes the goal easier to complete because you can break the work into increments. This helps the team early in their development to enjoy small successes while they develop and work toward more challenging goals. Writing out the steps helps all team members become *informed* about due dates and responsibilities.

6. Set up a system to measure progress.

The performance teams must have feedback on how well they are doing. Without knowing if they are progressing toward the target, the teams will not successfully accomplish the goal. Without feedback, it is tough to know if you are on the right track. Your teams should review progress on a weekly basis. The best way to review progress is to pick an item that can be measured. Examples could be parts per shift per labor hour, or number of defects as a percentage of production or cycle times. To keep up the momentum, take snapshots of little successes along the way as you begin to implement your vision. If your goal is to increase productivity by 20 percent, throw an informal party for the team to celebrate reaching the halfway point.

Kaizen

When performance teams follow the goal-setting process mentioned above, empowerment is created. Combine this process with a philosophy of continuous improvement — what the Japanese call "kaizen" — which starts with the realization that the improvement process is eternal, a way of life from now on. Kaizen is a Japanese term that defies a simple American definition. It means gradual, unending improvement of everything we do by using the power and knowledge of the people who are performing the operations. In other words, keep on improving the job, but do not dictate improvements. Ask the person who is doing the job to design a better way to do it. We achieve Kaizen, continuous improvement, through empowered performance teams that study their processes and keep score on certain measurables with an eye toward continually improving their score. There are no quick fixes or short-cuts for achieving long-term improvement, only the cumulative benefits that accrue to organizations committed to setting and meeting ever-higher standards.

Zero defects is a goal. But what does it mean? In the literal sense it means a defect-free product or service, but as a quality improvement slogan, it means the continuous drive to improve quality. And what this implies, of course, is KAIZEN: a never-ending need to make improvements a way of life.

Many people still believe that a certain percentage of all work must be defective. The concept of Acceptable Quality Level (AQL) was developed and widely adopted as a means for controlling quality. AQL is defined in the Statistical Quality Control Handbook as, "the maximum percent defective which will be considered satisfactory...and regularly accepted by inspection."

For instance, an AQL of five percent on incoming parts means that a shipment will be accepted if it has five percent or fewer defects. Although this standard may seem reasonable, accepting five percent faulty material has expensive consequences. Companies must hire people to sort out the good parts from the bad. Additional warehouse space and personnel must be hired to store, move and sort the material. People must inspect and test the product during and after assembly to detect faulty parts that weren't found during initial inspection. Space and personnel must be available for failure analysis and disposal of pumps with faulty parts, and the number of parts to be ordered must be increased by five percent to compensate for the expected faulty ones.

So AQL represents belief in the inevitability of errors. Your company can no longer afford this belief. Successful quality improvement programs focus on preventing and eliminating errors, not finding and fixing them.

The largest opportunities for improvement are identified, root causes determined, alternative courses of action evaluated, and controls put in place to maintain gains. This cycle of events demands the use of reliable methods for gathering, representing and analyzing *information.*

The new expected level of achievement for the performance team must become error-free work. Error-free work does not naively imply the need for perfection. Rather, it means we realize that errors aren't required to fulfill the laws of nature. When errors occur, their root causes are identified, and actions are taken to prevent them from recurring. In short, we no longer accept errors as inevitable, instead, we become dedicated to preventing errors.

* Knowing the destination means the team will enjoy the journey.

* Lay out a plan for setting goals.

* Strive for Kaizen, continuous improvement.

* Set a goal of error-free work.

* Shake things up; use new methods for achieving your goals.

Teaching

Then said a teacher, Speak to us of Teaching.
And he said:
No man can reveal to you ought but that which already lies
half asleep in the dawning of your knowledge.
The teacher who walks in the shadow of the temple, among
his followers, gives not of his wisdom, but rather of his faith
and his lovingness.
If he is indeed wise he does not bid you enter the house of his
wisdom, but rather leads you to the threshold of your own
mind.
The astronomer may speak to you of his understanding of
space, but he cannot give you his understanding.
The musician may sing to you of the rhythm which is in all
space, but he cannot give you the ear which arrests the rhythm
nor the voice that echoes it.
And he who is versed in the science of numbers can tell of the
regions of weight and measure, but he cannot conduct you
either.
For the vision of one man lends not its wings to another man.
And even as each one of you stands alone in God's knowl-
edge, so must each one of you be alone in his knowledge of
God and in his understanding of the earth.

The Prophet
Kahlil Gibran

>>>10

Tactical Training

*I will prepare myself and, when my greatest opportunity
comes, be ready.*

Abraham Lincoln

Kenny, a superintendent of a custom fabricating
manufacturing business, told our Leadership Development
LAB: "It was the summer break during my college days. I
was working at an aluminum fabrication company. I was hired
basically to help out in the shop, clean up work areas, the
typical grunt work college kids get hired for. I was excited
when I got the opportunity to help out one of the older veterans who was building a flatbed body for a pickup. He asked
me to cut out the decking. Although this was not a job requiring a lot of skill, I appreciated the opportunity to do something other than just sweeping floors.

I took out my tape measure and was getting ready to
measure the deck boards so I could cut them down to the
exact dimensions, when I noticed that 90-degrees of my tape
measure was loose. I just figured it needed to be fixed so I

took it over to the vise, got a ballpeen hammer and pounded down the rivets so the end would not slide back and forth. I went back to the deck boards and began to carefully measure them out so I could cut them to exact specifications.

After watching me for a few minutes and having a good laugh, one of the veterans came over and told me that I couldn't use my tape measure if I wanted an accurate measurement. He showed me that the end of a tape measure is supposed to be loose to allow for the 1/16th of an inch on the inside and outside measurements, depending on the application. I felt really stupid for not knowing how to correctly use a simple tool like a tape measure and heard about it several times from the more experienced workers for the next couple of weeks.

The lesson I learned from this experience is that even highly motivated employees need meaningful training to direct their inclination to peak performance. Letting people learn through trial and error is expensive. It can create scrap and can be very demeaning to self-esteem.

If you are committed to empowering your team, provide all the basic training. After each member of your team has mastered the basics of the primary job, begin a systematic approach to cross-training. The benefit you will gain is a fully empowered team that experiences the natural exhilaration that comes from learning and mastering new skills, and they will perform with excellence the first time every time. Your team will measure up, even in the toughest situations."

A 1995 study commissioned by the Labor Department found that investing in the work force boosts profits. Labor Secretary Robert Reich, who has often preached that employees should be regarded as "assets to be developed, rather than as costs to be cut," said that the study results can be a guide for managers who recognize the importance of continuously training the work force. The study found "real justification" for investing in innovative workplace practices, including not only training employees, but involving them in business decisions.

Midnight Oil

Betty, the operations manager of an emergency medical care service organization, told our Leadership Development LAB that Kim, a long-term co-worker, had been promoted from driving the wheelchair vans to graveyard dispatcher. One of her new responsibilities as a dispatcher was data entry. Over several weeks, it became obvious that there were some major problems with the quality and speed of this work.

"I decided to pull a graveyard shift with her, " Betty said. "I went in at 11 p.m. so I could provide some of the obviously needed additional training for this new dispatcher.

At the beginning of the shift, I was hearing 'I give up!' 'I hate this system,' 'They sure like to make it complicated, don't they?'

I said, 'Kim, let's go back to the basics.' And so we did. In just a short while, about an hour and a half, she had an entirely new expression on her face. I could see her confidence growing, and she started saying, 'Oh, now I see, this makes sense. Wow, this is going to make my job so much easier.'

There has been great improvement in both Kim's performance and attitude since I spent that extra time with her. The best part is, her reports have cleared up. They are on time and error free.

The lesson I learned from this experience is that I should never assume new people in complicated positions will master their jobs simply by doing them. Often, additional training is needed to perform with excellence.

As an empowering leader, it is my responsibility to ensure complete understanding of the team members' job requirements and equip them with all the skills and specialized knowledge needed to perform their tasks. I must pay attention to all team members, not just those who are easily and conveniently supervised. I cannot just leave them alone and hope things will work out. This is false hope."

When moving team members from one role to another, provide the empowering training needed. Pay attention and give the feedback needed to help them achieve outstanding performance. The benefit you will gain is an empowered team that consistently improves.

We often tell ourselves that we don't have the time to conduct training. Or maybe it just seems too expensive, especially if high turnover would render the training moot. Still, notice that even when we rationalize that there's no extra time to train while projects are in progress, we do, however, mysteriously find "extra" time to do rework. We pay the price of poor or no training when we remove or replace defective production or issue credit for defective service. Among the chief causes of turnover is inadequate training. People who experience failure feel inadequate and find little or no job satisfaction, naturally leading to turnover.

Around The Corner

Dave, a supervisor for an electrical contractor, told our Leadership Development LAB about how training — or lack of it — impacted his organization. He had climbed up in the rafters of a building to help Irving, one of his new apprentice craftsmen. Irving couldn't get a piece of conduit into the ceiling space. After Dave crawled up into the rafters, he realized that the conduit couldn't go in the available space with the 90-degree bend that it had. While Dave crouched on his knees, he sent Irving back to get a piece of conduit with the correct bend, about 30-degree — a bend that would go through the space available.

Dave was down on his knees waiting on the steel I-beam for what seemed like hours, long enough that it felt like the I-beam was starting to come up through his knees. The longer Dave waited, the more the pain grew and the more impatient he became.

Finally, Dave spotted Irving coming back with a piece of conduit which had the same 90-degree angle on it as the former piece. Of course, it was not going to fit through the available space.

Dave said, "I was biting my tongue. I wanted to say, 'How stupid can you be?'" He crawled back down off the I-beam to see what was going on, why this guy would come back with the same bend twice. He found out that Irving had never been trained on how to make the needed 30-degree angle bend.

What a vivid example of the high cost in time, productivity and frustration caused by inappropriate, incomplete, inadequate training! It has been conservatively estimated that our Japanese and German competitors spend two to three times the amount of money on training than their American competitors. Ideally, two percent of your budget should be devoted to training.

Before Nissan opened a truck plant in Smyrna, Tennessee, it spent the equivalent of $15,000 per associate employee on training. Similarly, when I heard the Executive Vice President of Motorola, Bill Smith, speak to over 300 of the top aerospace and electronic managers at Boeing in January of 1990, he was asked the question, "What did the training needed to win the Malcolm Baldrige award cost you?" He said, "I have no idea; no way of measuring what the training cost, but I think it cost us a negative $40 million." He went on to say that the actual out-of-pocket costs were about $4.5 million, but he was certain the company had saved at least $50 million.

My challenge to you is to honestly take a look at your attitudes and practices around training. Exercise the courage to ask your team:

> "In what one area would you like more training?"
> "In what one area do you think others in the company need more training?"
> "What training would you be willing to conduct?"
> "Would you be willing to come in before or after work for training?"

I asked managers at one company we were working with to report the on-the-job training they had conducted. I knew from conversations with the general manager that there was some procrastination going on around the assignment. Some class members were even implying there was no one for them to train.

On the morning of our session, which started at 7:00 a.m., all the class members, with one exception, gave a good report on the on-the-job training they had conducted. A few people admitted they conducted the training rather spontaneously earlier that morning before our meeting, since they began work at 5:00 a.m. The only person who didn't have a report to give was the corporate attorney, who said that unless they hired some additional lawyers there would be no one for him to train. I considered that a poor excuse, since there were clearly opportunities in this particular company to train people on issues regarding sexual harassment, separation policies and other legal aspects of supervision and personnel management.

At the close of the session, I drew three circles, each one inside of the other, on the board. I labeled the middle circle "core competencies," the second "job expansion" and the third circle "career development." I then went around the room and asked each person to tell me if they felt the training they had conducted was core competency, job expansion or career development. Over 70 percent of the class indicated the training they had conducted was basic core competency training. This was powerful evidence that there is a tremendous need to dramatically expand, enhance and strengthen our training practices.

Certainly, if our team members aren't trained in the core competencies, then there is very little chance we are going to compete successfully in the long-term. But we need to move beyond the basics. Every team member should be engaged in job expansion training and then take the opportunity to go on to career expansion development.

Train To Fit

Vern is the product development manager of a plant that manufactures household appliances. He told our Leadership Development LAB that a line chart measuring rejections was clearly illustrating a downward trend. Quality was getting worse, and there was a corresponding increase in rejects, rework and scrap. These errors were occurring in the manufacturing process of a new and improved damper system. The damper parts were not fitting together easily, if at all, when they arrived at the assembly department. Some had to be scrapped. Others could be made to fit if they went back to the forming department.

"I knew what needed to be done, and so I set up a time to train our press brake operators," Vern said. "Then I began planning my on-the-job training program. I knew the training would take about 75 minutes. I must tell you, I was nervous. I was way out of my comfort zone. Conducting on-the-job training was a brand new experience for me.

The first thing I did was give the operators praise for high quality they had been turning out on our other product lines. This helped relieve the tension, put everyone at ease, including me, and set the tone for the rest of the session. I went over the blueprints and hand drawings. Then I started the formal training program. First, I told them how to make the new part, as I made the part myself, showing them the step-by-step process. I then asked operators to perform the task, make the damper, as I told them step-by-step how to do it. Finally, I asked them to tell me how to make the part as they performed each step of the process.

Errors dropped and quality improved the very next day. Not only did productivity go up, labor and materials costs, as a percentage of sales, dramatically improved overnight. In effect, we had a double win. The sense of pride that comes only from achievement was owned and enjoyed by the operators.

The lesson I learned from this experience is the importance of meaningful, on-the-job training, and that for training to be empowering, the trainee must get hands-on experience and make the connection that comes when they repeat back and act immediately on what they have learned. The trainees must see me physically do the task as I explain it; must do it themselves while I explain the process; and must do it as they explain it to me."

Look at errors that are occurring in your organization, and then take full responsibility for the training of your team members. Carefully plan and enthusiastically employ empowering training and the job will be done right the first time. The results will be continuous improvements in quality, and increased customer satisfaction will be a new way of life in your organization.

The first step in determining training needs is to figure out what your team is required to know to do the job. Use the following questions to assist you in this:

1. How many people does it take to do the job?
2. How many tasks make up the job? What are the tasks?
3. How is each task accomplished? How many steps are there in performing the task? What is the order of the steps?
4. What tools, equipment or parts are needed to perform each task?
5. How does a person know when to start a task? What is the state of the product coming to the person? What does the person have to add to the product before it leaves their area? What makes the product complete?

6. If equipment is needed, how does it operate? How does the person start up, monitor, and stop the equipment?
7. What are the safety considerations?
8. What are housekeeping considerations in maintaining the equipment and work area?
9. How well must each task be performed?

Cheryl, a manufacturing service supervisor for a dental equipment manufacturer, told our Leadership Development LAB: "In March of 1995, I hired Alan as our new purchasing clerk for the dental furniture operation. Although Alan had past purchasing experience, I knew our systems were different than that to which he'd been accustomed. He also needed to learn our dental furniture product line, which was brand new to him.

I decided to develop a check-off list of all the duties involved in his new purchasing position. I knew this would allow me to stay on track as his trainer, and it would give Alan an easy-to-follow training outline. I know from past experience that an agenda or outline builds courage, confidence, and enthusiasm for the trainee. I used the Turbo Management System's Six-Step Process for On-The-Job Training to cover all of the important new duties listed on the job description check-off list."

Six Successful Steps To On-The Job Training:

1. Trainer Tells: What? How? Why?
2. Trainer Does.
3. Trainer Tells: What? How? Why?
4. Trainee Does.
5. Trainee Tells: What? How? Why?
6. Trainee Does.

"At the first step, I demonstrated and explained to Alan how to fill out our order forms, phone in orders and enter the information into the computer. Alan observed me as I explained and went through each step in the process slowly enough for Alan to feel comfortable and to allow him to ask questions as we progressed.

At the second step, I reviewed the same *information* with Alan, but this time as I explained the tasks, I asked him to input the work. I asked him to actually fill out the forms, phone in orders and enter the needed information into the computer.

At the third step of his training, Alan explained each step in the processes to me while he also did the work.

By following this process, I was able to complete the training procedures in less time, and I was much more thorough than I had been in the past.

The lesson I learned from this experience is the value of the six step instruction method. Following the six-step process required that I evaluate and really think about each step in the process. I had to think about what I do automatically and analyze the skills and knowledge required to be successful in each task. The process also helped me evaluate Alan's learning style and abilities. I found myself keeping pace with Alan's learning speed.

The actions I call you to are: 1.) Evaluate all of your training techniques; 2.) Make a list of all the knowledge, attitude and skills needed to be successful in every job in your department; 3.) Use the check-off list along with the Six-Step Process for On-The-Job Training model to train everyone on your team.

The benefit you will gain is a highly trained team of real pros. Your trainees will be more successful faster, and you will be a lot happier."

Your team needs to know how it rates in the four levels of competency in areas of performance:

Mastered. Completely skilled; in total control of this area of expertise.

Competent. Demonstrating adequate skill to succeed in this area of expertise.

In Training. Currently having a working understanding of the capability and what's missing in performance; also have a means of developing the capability in place.

Need Training. Currently do not have a working understanding of this capability or a means of developing this capability.

Then, ask yourself, as a leader, how trainable are you? How many books of preparation have you read this past year? How many improvement courses or seminars have you attended recently? Your greatest secret for success in the decades ahead will not be what you know today, but rather your ability to gather the knowledge necessary to bring your team into formation as it soars toward the future.

Who should do the training?

Using team leaders as trainers has several advantages:

1. They greatly expand your delivery capabilities, allowing training to take place sooner.
2. They can often be more effective trainers because of their ready ability to apply quality concepts to company-specific questions, issues and problems.

3. The quality message has more impact when people hear it from 'the boss.'
4. Team Leaders learn more about quality improvement by teaching it and, consequently, they are more likely to develop a feeling of responsibility for training and the quality improvement process.

Developing the instructional skills of your organization's team leader is where much of your early training will provide quick pay back. Training for quality cannot stop with the top management teams. Training must be extended to each individual contributor at all levels (machinists, programmers, engineers, etc.). Train first-level team leaders as trainers then charge them with providing their team members the knowledge and skills needed to fulfill individual quality improvement responsibilities. Quality improvement, like any major change in direction, is likely to have minimum effect unless front-line team members believe their team leaders support the changes.

When we teach someone else what we have learned, we learn twice: once when we receive, and again when we give. Receiving begins the learning process; teaching someone else completes it.

* Examine your attitude and practices toward training.
* Train to enhance quality and profit.
* Train to retain: Hands-on experience is critical.
* Train to empower both now and in the future.
* Train others to anchor your own learning.

Commitment

*is what transforms
a promise into reality.*

*It is the words that speak
boldly of your intentions.
And the actions which speak
louder than words.*

*It is making time
where there is none.
Coming through
time after time,
year after year.*

*Commitment is
the stuff character is made of;
the power to change
the face of things.*

*It is the daily triumph
of integrity over skepticism.*

>>>11

Keeping Commitments

The best of all leaders is the one who helps people so that eventually they don't need him.

Lao Tzu

Remember what happens when the lead goose tires? It rotates to the back of the *formation* and another goose flies to the point position. In organizations, as well, you cannot remain out in front forever. It pays to take turns doing hard tasks and sharing leadership with others. High performance organizations create a climate in which people eagerly fly to point position in their respective areas of influence. By contrast, imagine what would happen to the flock if the leader refused to relinquish any responsibility, but grew too weary to keep flapping its wings: Chaos!

Just before the first session of a new Leadership Development LAB, I ran across the parking lot to a nearby restaurant for a fast bite of dinner. I noticed a couple of loud guys as they sat down in a booth kitty-corner from me. They talked incessantly about their boss. The longer they talked,

the louder they talked. The louder they talked, the more pro-
fane they became.

It was obvious from the subject of their conversation
that they were contractors. Their main complaint seemed to
be that although they were the project managers in charge of
the success and profitability of their projects, and were responsible for bringing jobs in on time and under budget, the
company owner seemed to be making decisions about the
labor rate without consulting them. He was granting raises
without consistency, thus creating conflict between team
members. He would commit to one policy then turn around
and break his word. It appeared to be happening frequently.

Rather than empowering the individuals, the owner's
inconsistency resulted in a lack of dedicated teamwork and
confusion over accountability and responsibility.

As I observed this little drama play out, I noticed a
lady sitting in the booth next to them. She looked around to
see what was behind her, clearly upset by the loud profanity.
She picked up her place-setting and moved to another part of
the restaurant. Although there was no immediate way of knowing what company these gentlemen worked for, they certainly
did not endear the contracting profession to anyone who could
hear them.

As it turned out, those very project managers who had
complained so loudly in the restaurant were scheduled to start
my Leadership Lab that night. Although they had calmed
down somewhat when they arrived to class, it was easy for
me to see the frustration brewing just beneath the surface.
Yet, by the end of the first session, they were excited because
they saw that all the people present — including the leader
— would be held accountable to recognize how their decisions affected others. They were told we would examine the

consequences of broken commitments. The leader has a responsibility to think through how words and seemingly isolated decisions impact all areas of the operation. Before the second session, they asked us to come over to their organization and conduct an on-site workshop for their entire management group. We did, and the entire management team enrolled in the LAB, including the president of the company about whom they had been complaining.

They were all great class members. The project managers who once bemoaned their fate later became partners in the firm, and the company has gone on to record growth and profits.

Salvaged Opportunity

Jay, the president of a large holding company, told our Leadership Development LAB about an experience at his company's tube forging plant:

"While visiting with our materials manager, I learned the details of a proposed commercial transaction between our company and one of our competitors. The requirements being imposed by our competitor were of such an onerous nature that I developed a great concern that this transaction would ultimately prove to be very harmful to our company.

That afternoon, I expressed only the mildest concern to our materials manager, but the issue continued to bother me throughout the weekend. By Sunday night, I called the general manager and expressed to him in far greater detail the concerns that I had, posing to him a couple of alternative measures. I suggested we take it up both prior to and following the normal Monday morning staff meeting.

After the staff meeting I convened a meeting including the general manager, the plant manager, the materials manager and the quality assurance manager. I started the meeting by expressing very clearly my strongest reservations and concerns about this transaction. I then turned it over to the rest of the managers and provided them an opportunity to discuss the issue and come up with their own recommendations. The fellows came up with some really sound ideas which they have embarked upon with conviction and determination. They are turning a potentially negative situation into one that will no doubt become a positive arrangement for everyone.

In the past, I would have most likely come in Monday morning and told the materials manager to simply terminate the transaction. But I had made a commitment to let the teams in my company make their own decisions. If I simply squashed the entire plan, I might have saved some money, but I would have broken my commitment to the team and risked losing the trust of its members. In the long run, that would have cost me more. Since I was willing to listen to the team's ideas, we salvaged the opportunity for our company.

The lesson I learned from this experience is the importance of keeping commitments, even when you're tempted to step in and take over. Listening to the team's ideas and getting the perspective of all team members allow them to express their views and experience instead of my dictating an action.

The action I call you to in your pursuits of becoming an empowering leader is never prejudge the decisions of those persons you put in a position of authority. Always give them an opportunity to explain their full rationale for the decisions they have made, listen to their points of view, share yours, and allow for new decisions to be made. Remember, you will always have veto power, but exercise that veto power with the greatest of discretion. The benefit you will gain is an empowered team that will grow, develop and mature. Everyone on your team will be engaged in a continual learning process. You'll find that they are making more and more, and better and better, decisions every day. This will allow your company to grow and give you the freedom to go on to bigger and better opportunities."

Cleaned Up

Don, the project manager for a general contractor in Seattle, told our Leadership Development LAB he was having some real difficulty getting one of his crewmen to do the clean-up and closure at the end of each workday. Don wanted him to sweep and dust the hallways, turn on the dehumidifiers, open the windows slightly, and then turn on the heater before leaving. Don had told this crew member several times what he wanted him to do, but nothing was happening; the work was not being done. At best, the crew member was giving half-hearted attempts. He would make excuses, "I forgot to turn it on...I didn't realize you wanted that done...Oh, is that what you meant?"

So Don took him off to the side one day, where it was quiet, explained to him, again, slowly and clearly, not only what he wanted done, but why it was important. Don explained to him what happens in the curing process for varnishing, if the room is too humid or if there is a lack of circulation. He told the crew member, "You're in charge of the day's end clean-up and closure. I want you to know that I'm counting on you, and you need to take as much time as is necessary to complete your clean-up and closure assignment. If you need any extra tools or equipment or my support in any way, I'll get it for you; it's your responsibility to complete the job successfully. I want you to be fully responsible, and I am holding you fully accountable. Will you accept the accountability for having the hallways cleared, the dehumidifiers turned on, the heaters turned on, and the windows opened just a crack before you leave?" The crew member then said he would.

Don told our class, "Since then, everything's been done every day without a flaw or a hitch. I can see my crewman is taking more pride — more care — in his work. He seems to have a sense of ownership. Now that he sees the big picture and how important he is to the success of the project, he's even taking care of details I haven't thought about. I committed to empowering him. In return, he committed to doing the best job possible."

If you want to improve performance, enhance quality, eliminate re-work, shorten cycle time and finish projects on time and under budget, empower your crew by assigning responsibilities. Ask team members to accept accountability for their own work and help them see how their task fits into the big picture. In turn they will execute the job with ownership. Make your desired results clear, explain the parameters, and give your team power, authority, responsibility and accountability. It will take some of the burden off your back and free you up to do other assignments. You will be lighter, and they will stand taller. You will build a high-performance, winning team.

Who Will Do What By When?

Part of keeping a commitment is to make sure you have clear agreement on the task or issue with whoever else is involved. Commitments are breached and promises broken when one person fails to understand the nature of an agreement. Randy told the Leadership Development LAB: "It was the spring of 1983, and I was the pipe fitter foreman on an oil tanker that was sitting high and dry on the Portland docks. I had just received a new item of work to perform in the bottom of the pumproom. The job involved some cutting and welding on a crude oil cargo line. I went to the location of the ship where the task was to be performed. I was with the person who was going to accomplish the work. I instructed the worker to first drill a hole in the bottom of the cargo pipe, then have it 'sniffed' by the marine chemist to make sure it was gas free and safe to perform the hot welding. I then took a black felt pen from my pocket and drew on the side of the pipe an arrow pointing to the bottom of the pipe and wrote, 'Drill quarter-inch hole.' About three hours later, I was in my office having lunch when I received a phone call from the project manager. He had the marine chemist in his office. He said, 'There is an easier way to find out what the weather is like under the ship than drilling a hole through the bottom of the ship's hull.' I really had a good laugh until I saw the look on the worker's face. He was very quick to point out that he was wondering during the two hours it took him to drill through the two inches of steel plate, 'Why does this guy want me to drill a hole through the bottom of the ship?'

"The lesson I learned from this experience is the importance of making sure my instructions are clearly understood and always ask if there are any questions! (Of course I wanted him to drill up through the pipe!) Better yet, ask the other person to relate back their understanding of the project. Then ask them how they plan to go about the work."

Any time we ask others if they have any questions, we are likely to get a no response because we are putting the responsibility for understanding on their shoulders instead of shouldering the responsibility for understanding ourselves. Ask, "Have I made myself clear?"

Here is a 7-step model for empowering through assigning responsibility. The secret is up front, mutual understanding and commitment.

1. Tell <u>what</u> is to be done and what resources are available. Ensure that guidelines are clear.
2. Explain <u>why</u> and <u>how</u> the work fits in to the big picture.
3. Explain the desired results expected from the specific assignment.
4. Ask if the person accepting the assignment is willing to be accountable for the results.
5. Ask for the person's plan of action. For a simple task, an oral plan is all that is needed. The action plans will reflect just how clear your assignment has been.
6. Modify the plan if appropriate.
7. Follow up. The purpose is not for you to interfere or micro-manage, but to support, provide help and encourage.

Remember how disempowering failures can be to others. Help your team members find ways to be successful, and through the process, build people and make them successful. This is one of your most important skills as an empowering leader. You need not second-guess an empowered team. When your standards are clear and your team is flying toward its goal in harmonious *formation*, all members know the role they play in gliding toward your destination.

Aligning Agreements

You can counteract one poor communication habit by beginning to make clear requests and by allowing for negotiation. In making requests, the goal is to reach agreement between yourself and another party. That way the work is done and both parties feel rewarded. When making requests of a team member, you will reach agreement more often if you:

1. Be sure you know exactly what you want to communicate before you begin. (Indecision and confusion on your part create doubt and a lack of confidence.)
2. Consider the availability of team members' time and whether they are the ideal persons for the job. If their schedule is heavily loaded, give them the priority level of the work.
3. Present your request in a logical sequence and in a clear, concise language.
4. Use terms and language the recipient can easily understand. Recognize that some may not understand as readily as you do.
5. Ask rather than order. Be sure that there is no doubt about your request, and get a clear response.
6. Be considerate when asking that a job be done.
7. Talk deliberately. Avoid shouting across a room or making an unnecessary show of power. Save your power for such times when it is really needed. Otherwise you could reduce your effectiveness if you are unnecessarily forceful.

8. Take personal responsibility. Avoid quoting a higher authority to gain compliance or to relieve yourself of responsibility.

9. Give each team member the opportunity to ask questions and to express their ideas.

10. Follow up to make sure you were understood and that the task is being performed.

Remember, empowering leaders do not blame miscommunication on others. They accept the responsibility for a lack of understanding. A great idea is to double-check to be sure that the person you have made the request of understands you.

After conducting various surveys for a steel distributor, Turbo Management Systems formed a Quality Steering Team. The first assignment of the team was to prioritize the opportunities for improvement. Many problems surfaced in the Employee Opinion Survey, and additional problems surfaced as we continued our analysis of the company.

The major problems mentioned in the survey were lack of communication, lack of *information* and poor morale. Another problem, one that may seem trivial by comparison, was a lack of spare parts for trucks and the overhead crane. This resulted in down time on the overhead crane and created frustrations for everyone concerned. It was then difficult to meet customer demands and expected performance standards. It is disempowering to try to do your best with broken-down equipment when all it would take, in some cases, is a $6 light bulb to complete the task.

On the first day of the Quality Steering Team meeting, we looked at a list of over 20 opportunities and boiled them down to the top three which we agreed would be attended first. We agreed to go to work immediately to try to solve these three priority problems: 1) the communication problem; 2) the need for recognition, which was creating a lack of motivation; 3) the problem of unscheduled down time on equipment and the resulting impact on productivity and morale.

One of the first assignments was for the warehouse manager to get together an inventory of all existing spare parts. He agreed to do that by our next meeting scheduled for one week. At the next meeting, when it came time for his report, he had excuses - not enough time, and many emergencies that week. He even convinced me of his inability to complete his assignment. Again, he agreed to make the inventory list before our next meeting in two weeks. At the next meeting two weeks later, he still had not completed the inventory list. He had not followed through with his agreement. We pushed a little harder at this meeting and he told us he did not think it was really a problem, and we really did not need to pursue the parts inventory. We reminded him that in the minds of the customers, crane operators and truck operators, it was a problem. At that point he recommitted. This went on for two more meetings. When we finally got the spare parts inventory, we discovered there weren't any spare parts. The real reason he had been procrastinating on inventorying spare parts was because he didn't want to admit to the fact that there weren't any. The operators were right. The next step, of course, was to develop a list of spare parts needed.

In order for an organization to create breakthroughs, there has to be a willingness to deal with issues head on, make promises and be committed to keeping those promises. If team members verbalize agreements without real commitment, any quality improvement efforts will be stopped before they get started. The whole team will be let down.

As pointed out in the opening poem in this chapter, when you commit, you agree to do something specific, generally with expectations of success, improvement or excellence.

Agreements are truly the essence of teamwork; they move everyone in the same direction. They exist not only between you and your team, but between all the individuals and all the teams in the organization. When the organization is truly in alignment, these agreements are unspoken, because you have already agreed upon a shared mission and vision. You have agreed to work toward a common goal. Each team member in every team is accountable to one another for demonstrating the attitude, behavior and performance necessary to attain organizational success.

Don't Open With Excuses

I arrived early at a restaurant for my 7:00 a.m. meeting. I watched people come in for their breakfast appointments. I guarantee you, the most common greeting I heard was, "Sorry I'm late." It was a blustery morning, and traffic was moving slowly, so I suppose there were justifiable reasons for being late. It would not have been so bad if I had only heard one person say this, but as person after person came in, the accumulation of "Sorry I'm late" reminded me again that excuses never look good. (By the way, my appointment did not show up at all.)

Don't begin by making excuses. Even when agreements are broken, as they inevitably can be, the person responsible must recommit and take action to again bring the team back *in formation*. Remember, the empowered team does not try; it simply does.

* Breaking commitments affects the attitude of your entire team.

* Make specific requests and follow up to ensure you are understood.

* Let the team make decisions when you are tempted to take over.

* Ask team members to be accountable for their own work.

* Take accountability. Don't make excuses.

SAY WHO

Here in this team when we find
One of us whose work has shined,
We share their joy and let them know
How much their work has let us grow.
A word of praise — we pass it out
Where all can hear and all can shout.
In this team we often find
A Member whose work is the proper kind.
And whenever one has a fine thing done
We let everyone know "This is the One."
We go to them and smile and beam
And say, "This one is part of our team!"
A bit of praise has little cost,
But without due praise the team is lost.
There is never a one on this old earth
But is warmed to be told that they're of worth.
This team's bold world, when the work is good,
Is welcome and warming and well understood.
In this team we strive to cheer
When one of us has seen duty clear.
For one who gains their best each day
Has done far more than earn their pay.
They've earned our greatest thanks and trust
And Blessings — They're one of us!

-David, Leadership Development Lab Graduate

Embracing Encouragement

The more successful you are the more powerful your feedback will be to others — the more empowering you can be to others.

-Gary Zukav

Encourage Mints

Pete, the president of a medical services company, told our Leadership Development LAB about one of the most difficult people on his team. An ever-increasing distance had been developing between Pete and his afternoon-shift Driver Supervisor. Over several months, the supervisor had become disruptive and uncooperative. Pete decided upon a simple, proactive strategy to bridge the gap and re-establish the lost communication. He began by paying positive attention to this shift supervisor, and Pete made a deliberate point of simply saying "hello" to him whenever he came in for his afternoon shift.

After a few days, Pete began to visit with the shift supervisor and make small talk about the weather or traffic. As the days progressed, their visits grew longer and more substantive. Adding to the dynamic situation with his driver supervisor, Pete's General Manager had suffered a heart attack a few months earlier. After trying to return to work, the G.M. found he was unable to keep up the hectic pace and therefore resigned. Losing the General Manager left a tremendous hole in the operation that no one seemed willing or able to fill.

Pete began to look for the right person to replace the now-retired General Manager. The afternoon shift supervisor who had been his major problem actually began to take on some of the former General Manager's assignments, voluntarily, without direction or outside suggestion from Pete. He handled billing, reports, personnel records and miscellaneous paperwork.

The investment Pete had made in the past few months was simply one of paying attention, and the returns he gained far outweighed anything he could have anticipated. Notice how Pete started small. If people reject your approval, then you have not earned the right to ingratiate yourself with them all at once. Your motives will be questioned, and rightly so. Try what Pete did — start by first paying attention. Heaping praise on someone to whom attention has not been paid before is like skipping first base and running to second. You will never score that way. Effective attention is accomplished through warmly acknowledging, observing, and listening to others without judging them.

Pick a problem team member. Put together a proactive strategy for opening up communication, and start by paying attention. One of the ways we can empower the team, and express a belief in others, is by honking encouragement. Geese like corn and people like mints: encourage-mints. Pass these little "encourage-mints" out all day, every day. We may like the chocolate covered after-dinner mints, but our favorite mint is encouragement. The more you give out, the easier it becomes. Your capacity for giving encouragement expands, like your biceps expand with exercise. All members of the team must exercise encouragement if we are to achieve the 71 percent advantage. The skeptic, the cynic, the nay-sayer, creates a drag that holds back the entire team.

Provide Courage Through Encouragement

Encouragement literally gives people courage. To create an *in formation* team, we all must continually pat each other on the back. A few words of encouragement at a time of disappointment or in the midst of struggle may be worth more than a ton of praise at a time of success. It's so easy to find ourselves complaining about a person's performance rather than giving encouragement when the team member is really trying.

To create a championship team that flies *in formation*, we need to give encouragement. Our Employee Opinion Survey has shown repeatedly that one of the major complaints of the average employee is not pay or working conditions, but "I don't get recognized: The only time I hear from the boss is when things aren't going well."

Some managers have trouble passing out encouragemints. They pay a compliment as though they expect a receipt. Recognize good work and you provide the team the will to do better work. You become an empowering leader who wins more respect.

Public praise pulls people past previous performance. With praise, we can raise the team to new heights. Anything that is appreciated increases in value, and it could be said that an organization that expresses appreciation is one rich in human resources.

As people become more experienced and dependable, they require less attention, and leaders spend less time with the team. What sometimes results is that a barrier is erected, with leaders on one side and team members on the other. This doesn't happen just with unpleasant bosses. It can happen to the best intentioned leaders. You awaken to the fact that you are not in a close relationship with your team. The problem is simply lack of attention. When you or your assistants were new on the job, you made a special effort to get to know others. You tried to talk to them enough every day or so to keep track of how they were feeling, what they were doing. They appreciated this attention and interest. It developed a sense of togetherness and teamwork.

People are not machines; they need more than oil and grease and not only when they are breaking into a job or having problems. They like a show of interest and personal attention from the leader day after day, and they work better and enjoy their jobs more when they get it.

Take the time to just say hello. Give team members a chance to get things off their chests. Find out if they have had any personal problems or triumphs. Telling an empowering leader about something personal gives most people a tremendous sense of satisfaction.

Charged Up

Arlen, a car-battery distribution warehouse manager, told our Leadership Development LAB about Mike, a worker who had transferred from a slow-paced environment to a more efficient warehouse. "You could say, he had a habit of moving at about 30 percent of our pace, and seemed to like it that way. He had definitely become a product of his former working environment," Arlen said. "He showed up with the attitude that all he had to do was phone our customers and do the computer work. I explained to him that in addition to phoning customers for orders and entering the orders into the computer in the morning, he would also be pulling orders in the afternoon. Pulling orders is a part of the job Mike had not anticipated. He developed a bad attitude immediately and, of course, his bad attitude was influencing other employees. I tried several ways to get through to him, but he was not receptive. He was not happy with his added workload, and everyone at our location was made aware of it.

Then, on a Monday in early December we had an exceptionally busy day. We sold and shipped over 2,400 batteries that day, and everyone had to pitch in. Mike worked like I've never seen him work before. He pushed himself all day long. He set the tone, the pace, and the tempo for everyone else to follow. I got to work extra early the next morning and wrote a note of appreciation to our entire crew, complimenting a job well done. On the bottom of the memo I wrote a special thanks to Mike for being the instrumental pace-setter. I told him he was the person who helped guarantee our success. I hung the note on the time clock for everyone to see. Believe me, you could not miss it! That was a turning point for Mike in both attitude and production. He has changed dramatically and, I believe, permanently.

The lesson I learned from this experience is the power of praising people publicly (posting praise for peak performance). When people do well, tell them in front of the other members of the team. Put it in writing and post your praise for everyone to see. The benefit you will gain is increased team pride and an incentive for others to go the extra mile.

Merry Christmas

My wife and I attended the Annual Awards-For-Excellence Christmas Celebration held by one of our clients, conducted just a few months after the three owners of this firm graduated from our Leadership Development LAB. After dinner, David, the president of the company, stood in front of the group and began by presenting the first award for excellence. He named the recipient, named the award (Most Creative), and welcomed the recipient to the front of the room. When the winner reached the podium, David went on to give the specific incident that supported this recipient's creativity.

Then another member of the management team presented the next award for Most Determined. When the recipient arrived at the front of the room, a specific example was cited that supported the qualifications of the recipient for this award.

As the evening progressed, I realized that every employee of the company — 30 in all — would receive an award. Each award named a specific positive quality or trait that the recipient had displayed over the former year, and it was supported by a specific example.

I was astounded when they said that this year they were going to include "outside suppliers" in their awards. I, Larry W. Dennis Sr., President of Turbo Management Systems, was the recipient of the Most Inspirational award. They also presented a certificate to our sales associate, Steve Perry, for Best Client Service.

As the team members received their certificates, their emotions were apparent in their acceptance remarks: "This is the best company I've ever worked for. This is the greatest team I've ever been a member of. I love working for this company," and so on.

The evening was empowering for us all. It was certainly an anchoring event for all of the team members in the firm as they experienced recognition — the thing everyone wants and money cannot buy. The certificates were obviously crafted in-house and were small enough to print two per page, so it certainly was not the expense involved that resulted in the empowerment I witnessed.

Many organizations spend an inordinate amount of time and thought just planning the holiday dinner menu and miss the perfect opportunity for recognizing team members. It took courage for management to stand up and say, "We respect and admire you." It also took thoughtfulness to come up with 30 specific positive qualities accompanied by 30 specific examples to support those qualities to be accepted by the recipient as sincere.

The cynical reader may say, "I don't know if I could find a positive quality about each team member," or "I don't know if I could find a specific example that demonstrates that quality." I say the fault is probably not in the team member but perhaps in the cynic's own lack of vision or lack of attentiveness to the team. Some of us have an inclination to see the blemish. We let faults and errors build up in our mind and in our memories, obscuring our ability to truly see the positive.

If your team members are not displaying positive qualities and traits that could be supported by specific examples, then perhaps you should be looking for new team members. My guess is there are plenty of outstanding qualities in every person on your team. It's up to you to discover them.

My challenge to you is: Find dramatic ways to acknowledge and empower. You will have an empowered, dedicated, loyal, committed, enthusiastic team.

Sweatshirts

Ed, a superintendent with a major industrial construction company, told our Leadership Development LAB about how his organization's president brought out a box of newly designed company sweatshirts during a weekly meeting. The new sweatshirts had the company logo beautifully printed in contrasting colors on the front and back.

"He told our management team of superintendents and foremen that these shirts were to be awarded to those associates who were caught doing something extra, going the extra mile, performing at levels that exceed our customers' high expectations," Ed said.

"I was a little skeptical about how this would be received since only two of my 10-man crew could earn a shirt. When I made the announcement a few days later at my crew meeting, everyone was very excited. A few days later, when I did give out my allotment of two shirts, the guys who got them were pumped. Even the guys who did not get a shirt were excited by the recognition and the idea of rewarding superior service. I could see that this recognition was building *esprit de corps*, and I was pleasantly surprised.

The lesson I learned from this experience is that rewards and recognition work! I now believe that intrinsic recognition for any member of my team is a great motivation for every member of the team."

Accepting Praise

Sometimes it's easier to give than to receive praise, especially if you are already in a position of power. Tom, the president of a manufactured housing sales company, told our Leadership Development LAB about the time he went to his bank and congratulated the woman who had just been named vice president.

The woman, Dianne, said "Oh, it's nothing. It just means I get more dirty work to clean up."

"Dianne," Tom told her, "you are too professional to respond to a compliment that way." Her face turned a little red.

Tom said the two of them sat down to talk, and he explained to her the importance of handling praise with dignity. When you are given praise, awards, special presentations or a promotion, you can demonstrate your professionalism and further strengthen your image by following this easy three-step formula for accepting recognition:

1. Thank You. (That's easy.) Say it clearly, distinctly and with excitement. Name the person or organization who has granted the honor or the award. (Example: "Thank You, Tom. Congratulations coming from you means a lot to me.")

2. Recognize those who have helped you in your achievement. None of us can say that our achievements are a result of our individual efforts alone. We all have many to thank for the help they have given us along the way. Give your "team" the credit they deserve. You show your professionalism, strengthen your relationships, and enhance your image in the eyes of everyone. (Example: "My team deserves a lot of the credit. I couldn't have done it without the team's help.")

3. Tell what you will do with the award. This helps to add value to the award and shows appreciation to the person or organization that presented it. (Example: "I am going to pass your compliment along to my team.")

"Dianne was delighted and said no one had ever trained her in how to accept congratulations and praise," Tom said. "After I finished my business and turned to leave, she grabbed a co-worker walking by her. 'Tom, without this wonderful person's team support, I would not have been promoted to V.P.,' she said. 'Right on!' I said.

Three people were smiling in the bank lobby that day."

Mailing The Mailman

Dan, the production coordinator for a steel distribution center, told our Performance Team Management class about his wife, Michelle, an accomplished seamstress. "She makes an average of four wedding dresses a year for friends and other 'word of mouth' clients. One summer she was involved with making the wedding gown and bridesmaids dresses for Amy, a friend's daughter," Dan said.

"Amy insisted she had mailed all the measurements for the bridesmaids dresses to Michelle, but as the days rolled by, the *information* didn't arrive. Finally, about a week after we expected the measurements, they arrived in the mail. As soon as we looked at the envelope, we knew what the problem had been. Amy had addressed the envelope with not only the wrong street but the wrong zip code!

There was a short note from our mail carrier explaining that she was sorry for the delay, but it had taken her a little time to figure out where to deliver the envelope. Michelle was delighted. The measurements would have been very difficult to replace because two of the bridesmaids were out of the country and not expected back until just before the wedding. Naturally, it would have been difficult to make the two bridesmaids' dresses in the four or five days that would have remained before the wedding.

At my suggestion, Michelle wrote a note to our mail carrier thanking her for the 'beyond the call of duty, extra mile service.' The next day, we got a short note from our mail carrier thanking us for the acknowledgment.

We didn't think anything more about it until an official-looking envelope came. Our first thought was that somehow we had caused some trouble by writing the note and leaving it in the mailbox. We were both relieved and pleased when we opened the envelope and read a letter from the Director of the Post Office thanking us for our note to his employee. His letter went on to say that in keeping with his department's quality efforts, our mail carrier would be awarded a letter of recognition to be given in the presence of her peers.

As Michelle and I talked about it, several things came to mind. First, I think anyone who 'goes the extra mile' should be rewarded with the courtesy of a thank you. A written note takes a little time, but can have far-reaching benefits. At a

time when my own company was struggling to adopt the total quality concept, I was pleased to see that our Post Office
was working along similar lines. It meant a great deal to
Michelle and me that the manager of our Post Office thought
enough of our actions to write us a letter thanking us and
telling us what actions he would take to recognize his employee.

This all sounds like a big elaborate deal with letters
and notes going back and forth, but it really only takes a few
moments to acknowledge a job well done."

Writing a note of encouragement not only empowers
the recipient; it empowers you as well. Scott, executive vice
president and partner of a furniture retailer, noticed that one
of his sales associates had low morale and sales to match.
Scott wrote her an encouraging note. He wrote that the store
was pulling for her and that he knew she had the talent to do
great things. After she read the note the next morning, she
made a $6,000 sale with her first customer. She told Scott
that his note made the difference — giving her the encouragement needed to change her attitude and sell successfully.

Lyle is a project engineer for a paper mill. During a
construction project, an "eager beaver," one of Lyle's co-
workers who was not minding his own business, walked
through the project and made an "inspection." He was critical of a couple of areas in the project and reported the imag-
ined infractions to the construction company's superintendent. The superintendent was upset, and Lyle ended up getting an earful.

Lyle was upset himself because the eager beaver's
inspection was not appropriate in the first place. He calmed
down and debated how to handle the problem. He sat down,
took out one of the thank-you notes he had received in his

Leadership Lab, and wrote the eager beaver a 'Thank You.' Lyle thanked him for calling attention to the problem areas, and said he would appreciate being included in all future inspections. Lyle says that everything has worked out between the eager beaver and himself since he sent the note. Their communication has improved, and the surprise inspections have stopped. Lyle is sure he will be included should the eager beaver decide to conduct another one!

When you write encouraging notes, you bring happiness into other people's lives. You impact their mental attitudes. You brighten their day simply by writing a short note. Not only do you lift their mood, you are forming in yourself a powerful habit.

My challenge to you is to take the time, today, to write three notes. Put your thoughts of appreciation and gratitude in writing. Through the process, you will be lifted above pettiness, fear, self-centeredness and ego, and this lift will reflect in everything you do. There may be times when you will be sorry about something you said, sorry that you stayed too late or left too early, sorry that you won or lost, but all your life, you will never be sorry you were kind.

By taking the time to acknowledge others in writing, your team members will roll up their sleeves and go to work for you! There may be a little misunderstanding between you and some friend, team member, relative or loved one. I challenge you to write that person a note and ask for forgiveness. Even though you are not fully responsible, still ask forgiveness. It takes a big person to ask for forgiveness. You will not lose prestige. You will grow in stature.

Your three notes will take you about nine minutes. You can change, enhance, empower, renew three relationships. Start right now. You can fill in little "chunks" of time while you are waiting for appointments, on a plane, or even while waiting for meals.

When you give the most precious possession — genuine and sincere attention — you need not worry about dire consequences. It is a fundamental principle that goodness comes back to you ten-fold.

The fundamental purpose of a note is to remind other people that you are thinking about them. In these notes you express your appreciation. Do not ask for anything, only the privilege of their acquaintance. Do you remember how you felt when you received a note of appreciation, what a wonderful glow it gave you? Decide right now that you are going to give others that wonderful feeling by bringing them purposefully into your life through valuing them. We can never have too many friends trusting us, loving us and boosting us!

After actor/director Michael Douglas had been in five blockbuster films, his father, actor Kirk Douglas, wrote him a note. It said, "Michael, I'm more proud of how you handle success than I am of your success." This is a note Michael Douglas treasures.

The benefit you will gain from recognizing and rewarding extra effort is a proud, high performing team, a team that is proud to wear your organization's name.

* Pay positive attention to troubled team members.

* Provide courage with encouragement.

* Celebrate success.

* Accept praise gracefully.

* Write notes of acknowledgment.

Our deepest fear is not that we are inadequate.
Our deepest fear is that we are powered beyond
measure.
It is our light, not our darkness, that most
frightens us.
We ask ourselves, who am I to be brilliant,
gorgeous, talented and fabulous?
Actually, who are you not to be?
You are a child of God.
Your playing small doesn't serve the world.
There's nothing enlightened about shrinking
so that
other people won't feel insecure around you.
We were born to make manifest the glory of God
that is within us.
It's not just in some of us; it's in everyone.
And as we let our own light shine,
we unconsciously
give other people permission to do the same.
As we are liberated from our own fear,
our presence automatically liberates others.

From Nelson Mandella's 1994 Inaugural Speech

>>>13

Caring Coaching

An effective athletic coach must be a teacher, a psychologist, and a motivator. He must possess leadership qualities and, at the same time, he needs the confidence and concentration to operate at maximum efficiency under great stress.

-Tom Landry, former football coach, Dallas Cowboys

Building a championship team requires that all team members excel at giving and receiving coaching.

The new regional manager of a major flight services company told me he needed to make his operation profitable again. "Part of how I plan to do this," he said, "is through re-staffing. I've replaced one manager because, before I got here, 'the staff was tired of being bruised' in weekly meetings."

I said, "You mean, bruised egos?"

He said, "No, I mean bruised bodies, from sharp and blunt objects being thrown at them."

I know some people still manage through fear, intimidation, and in this case, violence. The manager hurling objects at his staff created an intolerable environment. An environment like this does not foster growth, change or improvement. The fear of another outburst squelches creativity and innovation. What is equally unfortunate is the destructive behavior presented over time through the intimidating influence of the manager. I would like to think the day of the bully-as-coach is gone. When this kind of unacceptable outburst are allowed, everyone suffers.

The kind of directing that tries to frighten players into changing behavior does not work over the long haul, and does little to bring a team into formation. Manipulation, including naming, blaming and shaming, cannot be tolerated. If we resort to diminishing manipulation because we lack the skill to motivate or when we have no respect, no regard, no real interest in team members we may get short term results, but we will build long-term resentment! People will work at cross purposes, flying totally out of *formation*. We will never secure dedicated, creative, involved team members. We may enlist their backs but not their brains.

Caring coaching is encouraging, uplifting and expansive. To thrive and stay alive in these competitive times, tap positively the talents of your team. The pay-off to successful coaching is motivated players who sustain peak performance. The motivational coach knows there is a direct relationship between how people feel about themselves and how they perform. As a coach, you build self-esteem by praising improvement and listening to the team's concerns.

Remodel

Kim, a project manager for a general contractor, told our Leadership Development Lab about Rod, a project superintendent, who was scheduled to start on Phase II of a major office addition and renovation. This was no easy project, and three months before the scheduled completion date the plans for the renovation were non-existent.

"Rod knew it was going to be an extremely tough project and was skeptical about completing it on time. To make matters worse, Phase I, which we had just finished, had been nothing but problems, problems, problems," Kim said.

For example, overhead doors were delivered four weeks late, the painting subcontractor had a bad attitude and the drywaller whined incessantly. The quality of the subcontractor's work was very poor. Rod's level of enthusiasm hit rock bottom. Kim decided it was time for some motivational coaching.

"I decided Rod's enthusiasm level had to be raised before entering into Phase II," Kim said, "so I set up a private meeting with him in my office. The first thing I did was to be genuinely interested in the problems he had encountered in Phase I. Then I asked him what he could foresee happening in Phase II. I listened to his concerns, without interruption, as he went on and on.

His concerns seemed to all boil down to two main areas: Subs and Schedule. The sub issue was resolved easily by allowing Rod to choose the subs he wanted to work with. I had completed the schedule the night before and knew it was nearly impossible, so when I showed it to Rod I appealed to his high ideals. We worked through the schedule item by item, getting his ideas and all the 'Yes' responses that I could muster. I also made it clear what I felt needed to be done, as well.

Rod began to see and believe that he could, indeed, be successful with Phase II of the project. He walked out of our meeting with a renewed belief in himself and a fresh enthusiasm for our company and his project. Every week Rod enthusiastically informed me of being right on schedule, and that his subs were all doing terrific work.

Rod successfully completed a very tough job, and, more importantly, he had a good time while doing it. His enthusiasm turned a nearly impossible project into a winner for everyone."

Secrets Of Caring Coaching

Kim's coaching utilized many of the six critical factors that motivate team members to improved performance:

1. **Ask for performance.** Describe how the job is being done now, and then how you want it to be performed — what excellence looks like in the job. Then ask for the team members commitment to meet your expectations for excellence.

2. **Use personalized, positive reinforcement.** Do not take acceptable work for granted. Thank people for it. Praise them every time they improve.

3. **Build relationships.** This means treat your team members like real, human beings. That's what they are, and they respond best when your actions show you respect their individuality and you trust their intentions.

4. **Understand your team member's point of view.** Make a habit of listening to your team members and asking their opinion before you give directions or offer advice.

If you listen first, with an open mind, people are more likely to cooperate if you decide something must be done differently.

5. **Model what you want.** Approach your own work with a sense of urgency, use your time efficiently, and meet the goals you set. Show members, by your actions, that the job really does matter, that quality is important and deadlines are real.

6. **Refuse to accept poor performance.** Though textbooks on motivation seldom admit it, empowering leaders do tell team members when their performance is not acceptable. Sometimes this means a reprimand or better coaching. Either way, you are demonstrating that standards matter, and that, in itself, is motivational.

The Extra Mile

Imagine there is a nail in the company parking lot. Some people pick it up automatically. No one says they have to, but they would hate to see someone else get a flat tire. Others will not pick up the nail because that is neither their job nor their problem. Such actions will not help them get a raise. Your job, as coach, is to instill the kind of motivation where all team members will pick up the nail and go the extra mile for the team. They willingly go the extra mile and volunteer to help, because they know they are working toward a greater good.

Danny, the afternoon shift manager of a glass tempering firm, told our Leadership Development LAB about a customer who called in after the office was closed. The customer wanted a special order for the following morning. Instead of saying, "I'm sorry, we're closed; you'll have to call

back tomorrow morning when someone from customer service is here," Danny volunteered.

Danny jumped into action and made the calls necessary to get the final approvals and then started the process to
complete the job. The windows the customer wanted went to
crating the following morning, on to shipping, then out the
door before noon the following day. The customer received
the emergency shipment of windows in time, and Danny's
company cemented its vendor/partner relationship with this
client.

This proves once again that for us to achieve the kind
of superior customer service necessary to compete in an increasingly competitive world, we need volunteers. We need
people motivated to go beyond their job descriptions in order
to benefit the team and customers. Enlisting volunteers for
excellence is the role of empowering leaders. How good are
you at pumping up your team for the long haul?

In the past, managers gave orders, saw to it that they
were followed, and held people accountable if they didn't
comply. Managers earned their salaries by being in charge
and controlling what happened in their areas to guarantee
desired results. If they delivered the goods their bosses expected, they got nice bonuses and promotions.

All that has changed. A manager's job is no longer
that of a watchdog, police officer or slave-driver. Increasingly, today's empowering leader is a coach, facilitator and
cheerleader. Our main concern is how to shape a more supportive work environment and to find ways to help each team
member be more productive.

A Pinch In Time

Judy, a manufactured homes salesperson, told our Leadership Development LAB about how she learned to get all the facts before taking action. "Even though this incident happened over 15 years ago, it is still as fresh in my memory as if it had happened yesterday. We were living in Bend, Oregon, at the time. It was one of those perfect eastern Oregon summer days. I had just parked my car and was heading into a nearby convenience store when I was pleasantly surprised to spot my husband. He was making a call from an outside pay phone. His back was toward me, so I could not see his face, but I knew it was him because of his distinctive western clothing. He always wore blue jeans, cowboy boots, a blue shirt, tan vest and a 10-gallon western hat.

Feeling somewhat devilish, I decided to sneak up on him and give him a pinch on his rear. So I quietly, cautiously sneaked up behind him and gave him a big full-handed squeeze. Imagine my surprise, that quickly turned to embarrassment, when he turned around to face me and I realized it was not my husband but instead, a complete stranger. My face turned red. I said 'Oops, you're not my husband,' then I ran inside the nearby store. When I got safely inside, I burst into laughter. I couldn't believe what I had done.

The lesson I learned from this experience is the importance of getting all the facts before reaching a conclusion and taking decisive actions that require risk. I learned not to base my conclusions on outer appearances and assumptions alone.

Thoroughly investigate the situations in your life that seem to call for action before you act. Do not make final judgments or construct tactical action plans based on outer appearances alone. Get the facts, all the facts, before you make your final judgments, and before you take committing action. The benefits you will gain are actions that count, actions that move you in an upward progressive direction. All of your surprises will be pleasant surprises, and your laughter will be based on the joy of successful achievement."

This incident from Judy's life reminds me how easy it is to put people in boxes, to make judgments and to put labels on people that limit them, hold them and the whole team back. Any time we say, or even think "he always" - "she never" - "you can't expect them to," we have set up limits, the boundaries, beyond which they and the team cannot exceed. We have, by our thoughts and words, set up the limits of the team. Check out how many people on your team you have branded in limiting ways.

The next time you start to think or say a limiting, labeling, branding comment about a team member, PINCH yourself. Wake up to how you could hold back performance, and how embarrassing that can be. You will wake up the team and achieve peak performance.

Pulling Teeth

Glen, a dentist, told our Leadership Development LAB that his offices had an extremely high turnover rate in the reception position.

"Our receptionists average less than six months on the job before leaving. There is a constant need for training in this position. The more training we conducted the more it seemed the receptionists became de-motivated and the faster they seemed to leave," Glen said.

"Since the person in the reception position is the lifeline of a dental practice, I knew I had to do something. I began to use Turbo's three steps to effective coaching:
1. Point out what is being done well.
2. Pick one opportunity to improve performance.
3. Assert your belief in the team member's ability to be a peak performer.

I applied the three steps with lavish praise. I resolved to look for any and every opportunity to praise our new receptionist. The results have been outstanding. We have had a dramatic increase in new patient flow and significantly, measurably better staff rapport.

The lesson I learned from this experience is that praise is powerful motivator. It's infectious. In any medical profession we usually want to avoid infection; however, this is the kind of epidemic we need to start, and spread — an epidemic of supportive coaching with enthusiastic praise."

Look for those qualities in your team members that can be positively recognized and enthusiastically praised. You'll not only boost morale, you will create a more pleasant work environment that reduces turnover and attracts new business.

'But' Method

The 'but' method of coaching is very common, but it's not a very effective tool for improving performance or morale. In fact, it can do more harm than good. The 'but' method is complimenting an employee and then adding a caveat that tends to wipe out your praise. "You did a great job stacking the equipment, BUT, you put it all in the wrong place. You stacked the wrong equipment and you should have been

outside unloading the truck instead. The employee feels manipulated rather than empowered.

Tom, a purchasing manager for a heating, ventilating
and air conditioning company, told our Leadership Development LAB about how he avoided the temptation to use the
'but' method of coaching. He had received some small-di-
mension copper tube in bundles wrapped with filament tape
in the middle and on each end. (Filament tape is used because it is very sticky and durable. It takes a sharp knife and
a lot of effort to get it off.)

"My instructions to my warehouseman were to de-
band each bundle and put it in its respective, well-labeled
storage slot in the copper tube rack. I came back awhile later
and noticed he had put the copper tube in the correct bin areas, however he had failed to remove the sticky filament tape,"
Glen said.

"Rather than using the usual 'but' method, I decided
to utilize the Turbo method of validating the employee's ideas.
I had him help me pull a copper tube order, making sure he
pulled the tubes that he had incorrectly racked with the filament tape remaining.

As he struggled at pulling a tube out of the rack, I
asked him what he thought was causing him to struggle. He
told me the filament tape was sticking to the sides of the tube,
making it difficult to slide the tube out of the rack. Then I
asked him what he thought we could do to solve the problem.

He responded, 'If we completely remove the filament
tape the tubing will slide out much more easily.' I agreed and
told him that was an excellent idea. When I got back from
lunch I noticed he had removed all of the filament tape from
every bundle.

The lesson I learned form this experience is that rather than using the disempowering 'but' method, I could correct performance by using the leadership principles and the proper correction procedure together, and when my team discovers problems and solutions on their own, with a little guidance, the team is committed to implementing those solutions.

The action I call you to is don't react too quickly when a performance correction needs to be made. Instead, let team members utilize their own ideas as you make the necessary correction. Through this process you will coach your team to peak performance. Team members will feel enthusiastic about their work processes and experience the feeling of knowing they are a significant part of your team."

When a team is committed and in true partnership, people respond to coaching. There is an ongoing respect for the progress of the team and the best interest of each individual, even when that individual flounders. When team members feel motivated by coaching, they will be free to stretch and try new ways of performing tasks. Inevitably, they will fall short on occasion. As a coach, you can respond in a variety of ways:

#@&*!

Gerry, a computer engineer, told our Leadership Development LAB, "A few weeks ago, after hearing my 7-year old daughter blurt out yet another profanity, I decided the vocabulary being used by her and my 4-year old was bad enough for my wife and I to take some corrective action. I guess they had picked up these undesirable words from school, TV and the neighbors. I know they had never heard my wife or me use them.

We had made some previous attempts to correct and control the words the kids were using, but our efforts were not consistent or well-defined. I proposed a dramatic plan to my wife. We would work with the girls to make a list of forbidden words. The completed list of forbidden words would make the standards clear. We would then give each of the two girls five nickels every Sunday. Every time they said a forbidden word they would lose one nickel.

We sat down with the girls and asked them for their suggestions of words that really don't sound good, words that could make others uncomfortable, that they would try to avoid. They had a lot of fun thinking of these words and saying them for the list. We had a little debate about some words we wanted on the list, but the girls did finally agree to all the words we wanted, words better left out of our home. They had a good laugh as they had me repeat out loud the final list.

At the end of the first week, the girls did not have many nickels left, only four between the two of them. The second week they did better and by the third week both girls had all five of their nickels. In just three weeks we had cleaned up the language in our house, formed some new speaking habits and had a lot of fun along the way."

The same rules apply to coaching adults:

1. Standards must first be clearly defined.
2. Everyone who is part of the execution must be a part of creating the agreements.
3. To create new behaviors that require changes in habits, there needs to be consistent follow-up to ensure conformance to requirements.
4. Finally, rewards for improved performance must be available.

Involve everyone on your team in creating clear standards for all important performances so the team knows exactly what is expected in all areas of performance. Create your own incentives, recognition and rewards system and be consistent in your administration of your feedback and rewards system. Be sure your follow-up is timely. Tabulate and report results immediately. Soon everyone will live up to high standards and all of us will have more nickels in our pockets.

Sub-Contractors

Natasha, the customer service project coordinator for a manufactured housing distribution center, told our Leadership Development LAB about a call from a new customer asking if his home set-up was still on schedule.

"I replied with an enthusiastic 'yes,' and told him that the next step, installing the carpet in his home, would be the following day. He then informed me that the previous step (sheet-rocking) hadn't been started. I said I would check on it and call him back.

I called the contractor, told him of my conversation with our new home owner. I explained how it felt to be told by our customer that we did not know what was really happening in the final stages of completing his home. I asked him why the sheet-rocking had not been completed on schedule. He told me he had run into a problem the previous week and that his crew was on its way to the job 'today.' I explained the importance of letting me know if and when he was not going to complete a job as scheduled. I explained the macro process his micro process is a part of, the series of events that follow and precede his drywall work. I explained how the process is scheduled, and pointed out to him that if one aspect of the set-up is off schedule, the ramifications are enormous. I couldn't see his face, but I know he was taken aback. He said very little.

Later that afternoon, the contractor called me back and asked if there was anything he could do to make up for having let us down. (He was, I am sure, a little embarrassed, and had been somewhat defensive when I first called him.) I told him that I may have other jobs to assign to his company, but only if he would promise me to do the jobs on time when scheduled. He promised to tell me if a problem did arise, so I could keep our customers informed and make other arrangements, if necessary.

The lesson I learned from this experience is that I can, and do, empower others when I help them see how their work fits into the larger scheme of things. When I take appropriate corrective action, people do respond in ways that help us all grow, improve and perform at higher levels.

The action I call you to is make sure that everyone on your team understands the context of their work, the big picture, the whole system. Don't be intimidated by the idea of correcting someone. See the importance of correction, and understand that correction is a tool of empowerment. The benefit you will gain is a seamless organization and smoother sailing in all your undertakings. Your projects will come in on schedule, and your customers will be wowed by your pristine performance."

Review

Coaching can mean communicating the precise rewards your team members receive for meshing their goals with the organization's. The performance review can be the perfect opportunity for motivational coaching to bring the team's agenda into alignment with organizational goals.

The five points of an empowering review include:

1. Identifying job responsibilities.
2. Setting goals with measurable results.
3. Praising accomplishments.
4. Clarifying the team member's personal goals and agenda.
5. Synthesizing personal and organizational goals.

This process requires that you take the time to really know every team member personally, so you can draw forth the excellence they desire to express. Building an extraordinary team is a complex craft requiring sophisticated people skills. What is at stake? Profitability, company growth, satisfaction and security. We get what we want by ensuring that all team members get what they want.

Many Faces of Feedback:

Selecting:	Choosing team members for best fit.
Training:	The process of equipping team members to succeed.
Coaching:	Provided when people are attempting a task. They are early in their practice of a performance, or endeavoring to learn a new skill, ability or task.
Correcting:	When a person has completed a performance and has done so unsuccessfully. This corrective action normally includes coaching.
Encouragement:	The act of providing that which stimulates others to provide continual effort.

Reprimanding: When a person has been trained and demonstrates a competence or proficiency in a skill and has chosen not to perform as agreed.

Wandering Around

Observation is a key aspect of effective leadership. Of course, it goes without saying, you cannot observe much if you cement yourself to your chair. In our leadership training, we recommend "management by wandering around," that is, spending time with your team members while they are actually working. Marci, the manager of a sporting goods specialty store, told our Leadership LAB that she had made a beeline for her desk every morning for 10 years. "I would then work my way through endless piles of paperwork and other small tasks, hoping that when I finished, I would have time remaining to spend with my associates, department managers and floor people. The reality was that by the end of the day, I still had not found the top of my desk."

Marci decided to make a change. She walked into the store each morning, looking for good things her crew had accomplished in the previous 24 hours. "Now, as our day team arrives, I acknowledge their efforts, comment on successes, and give praise where it's deserved. Praise is much more enjoyable to receive when people know I have taken the time to really notice contributions first-hand. This also gives my team members an opportunity to express their concerns to me first-hand. They seem to feel more empowered, knowing that I seek opportunities to see them on a daily basis."

Marci learned that she can only understand the world of her team members if she gets out and operates in it. "Break up your old routines," Marci suggests. "Get out from behind your desk and out of your comfort zone. Mix in with your team. Look for the good your people do, and be the first to acknowledge it." You will earn the respect of your team. Your observations will be keener, and you'll be able to provide the constructive feedback that brings the team into even stronger alignment.

While providing feedback, consider:

1.   Is your feedback specific rather than general? It's more effective to tell a person, "Just now you were not listening to what the others said, but I felt I had to agree with your arguments or face attack from you," rather than tell a person, "You're dominating."

2.   Is your feedback focused on behavior rather than personality? It is important that we refer to what a person does rather than who that person is. It is more useful to say that a person "talked more than anyone else in this meeting" rather than referring to an employee as a "loud-mouth." The first statement allows for the possibility of change; the second implies a fixed personality trait.

3.   Does your feedback consider the needs of the receiver? Feedback can be destructive when it serves only our own needs and fails to consider the needs of the person on the receiving end. It should be given to help, not hurt. We too often give feedback because it makes us feel better or gives us a psychological advantage.

4.   Is the feedback directed toward behavior that can be changed? You increase others' frustration when you remind them of some of the shortcomings or physical characteristics over which they have no control.

5.   Is the feedback solicited rather than imposed? Feedback is most useful when the receiver asks the questions that those observing him/her can answer.

6.   Does the feedback involve sharing *information* or giving advice? By sharing *information*, we leave people free to decide for themselves in accordance with their own goals and needs. When we give advice, we tell them what to do, and unless asked, this is a burden.

7.   Is the feedback well timed? Generally, immediate feedback is most useful. The reception and use of feedback involves many possible emotional reactions. Excellent feedback presented in front of an audience may do more harm than good.

8.   Is the feedback limited to one or two specific areas that need improvement? To overload people with feedback is to reduce the possibility that they can effectively use it. When we give more than can be used, we are more often than not satisfying some need of our own rather than helping someone else.

9.   Does the feedback offer assistance or analyze the receiver? Answering the 'why' takes us from what we observe to the land of inferences and assumptions. Guessing at people's motivations or intentions tends to alienate them and increase resentment, suspicion and distrust; it does not contribute to learning or development. It is dangerous to assume that we know why people say or do something, or what they are "really" trying to accomplish. However, if we are uncertain of others' motives or intent, this uncertainty itself is feedback and should be revealed.

As you endeavor to empower others, I urge you to choose carefully how you give feedback to your team. Pick and choose your time so that your feedback will be accepted.

When you identify, understand and act upon the needs and expectations of the team. Everyone works in a way that keeps the organization *in formation*.

* Think before you coach.

* Three steps to Caring Coaching:

* No "Buts."

* Make it fun.

* Always focus on behavior.

MISTAKES

M ake

I t

S imple

T o

A dmit mistakes &

K eep

E veryone

S traightforward and honest

$$>>>14$$

Courageous Correction

Rewarding only past success exposes an organization to
failure.
It stifles risk-taking.

Bob Gary, Texas Utilities

Fault Finding

Lisa, the accounts manager of a heating, ventilation and air conditioning company, told our Leadership Development LAB:

"I was under the gun to close out the accounting books for both of our service franchises. I had run the preliminary reports and just needed to balance the inter-company accounts with our controller. I had met with him the previous day to close out the Portland office. The books were not in balance. The controller reassured me by saying that since the office had a new computer system, he was sure it was an error in their books. As I left his office, the owner of our company, Jay, stopped me and asked for the profit numbers, which I gave him with a passing comment that after the controller fixed his error, I thought we would have a great month.

The next day when the controller and I met to close out the Olympia office, we were again out of balance. The controller felt it must be in payroll and instructed me to have Pam, the payroll clerk, get me the correct reports. So I went to Pam and told her that her reports were no good and to give me new ones that were accurate. She graciously ran new reports and we proceeded to re-check all of the numbers. Everything looked fine except that the salary amounts were still all wrong.

I made a comment about wishing she could give me a report that showed the auto reimbursements separately. She looked at me and said, 'You didn't deduct that amount from salary, did you? This new system doesn't do the auto expenses that way.' I looked at her and said, 'Oh, no! I had just assumed the auto expenses would be treated the same way it was in the old system.'

So, not only was it my error, an error I was quick to blame on our payroll clerk, I had to go into the president's office and tell him about my mistake and also tell him that we didn't make the profit I thought we had.

The lesson I learned from this experience is the importance of making sure all of my facts are correct before assuming someone else's *information* is wrong. I learned to be very careful about blaming others for what looks wrong.

The benefit you will gain is less wasted time looking for the errors of others that may not exist. You will remain in your circle of influence, that which you can affect; you will stay out of your circle of concern that you cannot directly influence, and you will be an empowered person."

Candy Bar

Mike, the operations manager for Nabisco, told our Leadership Development Lab what happened when his 12-year-old son was arrested for stealing a candy bar from the neighborhood grocery store.

"When I got to the police station to pick him up," Mike said, "there he was in the back room, his head hanging low, with tears running down his cheeks. I didn't say a word to him during the long drive home. I was biting my tongue, really wanting to climb all over him, 'Why would you do a thing like that? You know how that makes me feel? What is your mother going to think?' But, he was being so hard on himself and felt so bad that I just couldn't make him feel any worse.

When we got home, I asked him to go to his room and write me a letter telling me how he felt about what he had done. He wrote a beautiful two-page explanation letter and brought it out to me. (I'm saving his letter to give back to him some day when he becomes a father.)"

It's easy to kick people when they are down. Attacking the person may compensate for our lack of confidence, but succumbing to this common temptation denigrates and disempowers others. When people feel under attack, they become defensive. We distance ourselves from those we are supposed to lead.

"The lesson I learned from this experience," Mike said, "is that when people make mistakes that are obvious, they are often harder on themselves than I could ever be on them. The action I call you to is don't point out obvious failures, or rub their nose in their foul-up. Allow others the appropriate opportunity for introspection and the development of their own action plan to correct the situation. The benefit you will gain is a quick response team made up of people who quickly regain their self-esteem, and you'll be respected as a caring leader."

Empowering leaders who help others save face develop a team of thoughtful players who make fewer mistakes. By allowing team members to be introspective, you gain the respect of your empowered team, and they break through to levels of higher achievement.

Two Ways To Correct

You can correct with brute force, or you can stop to consider how you may have contributed to an error. Here are two stories showing different approaches to correction. In both cases, mistakes resulted because the team members had not been trained.

Greg, a superintendent for an electrical contractor, told our Leadership Development LAB about the time he had just started a new job.

"I was sitting at my desk with my back to the door when, without any warning, the purchasing agent burst into my office with an order I had asked him to price out. He flung it down on my desk, and with a clenched fist, started to shout and cuss at me saying, in so many words, 'This is NOT the way these orders are done! Not before, not now, not ever!'

Before I could even think of how to respond to his outburst, he turned and stomped out the door, loudly slamming it behind him. At first, I could only sit for a few minutes, dumbfounded at the way I had been treated. It wasn't long before I decided that I would NOT accept his inappropriate action.

I picked up the order and went after him. I took him aside, making sure that I was out of earshot from the other employees, and I calmly explained that I was sorry the order was not to his liking. I told him I would appreciate a detailed explanation of what he expected to see from me. I also made it clear to him that I did not appreciate being treated disrespectfully, and I expected an apology.

He said, 'Okay, I'll show you the right way we fill out purchasing orders here at our company.' After he showed me how he wanted them written out, he then apologized. I said, 'Fine. I can do it your way, no problem!' All I needed was to clearly understand the standards (as he perceived them) to know what he wanted.

The lesson I learned from this experience is that unacceptable behavior from fellow team members should be challenged and corrected, not just tolerated. When I have the courage to confront, in a positive way, I find permanent solutions to problems.

The action I call you to is to be sure to have clearly defined procedures in place and to properly train everyone on the commonly used forms. Uniformity will prevent mix-ups and upsets in the first place. The benefit you will gain is every person in your company will treat each other as they would like to be treated when all employees are playing by the same set of rules. In essence, you will have an empowered team."

This story illustrates the breakdowns that occur when we fail to define, clarify, document and train to standard policies and procedures. The solution is to define standard processes and procedures wherever possible. If uniform procedures are not in place, assumptions will be made by the person who is responsible for the end result. Too often the consequence of these assumptions will be upsets and rework.

I challenge you to engage your team or everyone in your company in a study of all your processes. Make your analysis with an eye toward streamlining your processes and you will shorten cycle times and increase accuracy, productivity and customer satisfaction. Your strong, empowered team then gains a competitive advantage.

Bid Day

Stan, project manager for a major general contractor, told our Seattle Leadership Development LAB that his firm had tremendous turnover with its front-desk telephone receptionists, and on hurried bid days, all the calls were being forwarded to him. When he could take the stress no longer, he put his phone system on 'Do Not Disturb.' The reason Stan received all the calls was because his name appeared on the 'Request for Bids' section of the company's project list. Many of the aggressive subcontractors were asking for him by name as if they were old friends, rather than saying they were calling in reference to a bid. The operator was overriding Stan's 'Do Not Disturb' request and sending him all the calls.

At one point, Stan was about to go through the roof. He jumped up from his desk and walked out — ready to throttle the receptionist. Just before he got to her desk, he thought to himself, "She probably has never been trained. She has never been given clear instructions on what to do when subs called on bid days." He was sure she had never been trained, and in fact, he didn't even know if a company policy existed regarding the routing of calls for this kind of situation. Instead of blowing up, he walked out to her reception desk and said, "On the hurried bid days, when the subcontractors or anyone asks for me, what I'd like for you to do, if I've put the phone system on 'Do Not Disturb,' is collect the messages. I'll call them back as time permits." She said, "Fine." The interruption problem was solved.

This story illustrates the importance of giving precise directions and making our expectations clear. It is impossible for people to read our minds and perform in the exact manner we expect and need. I have heard similar examples time and time again.

An employee who has been with the organization for years is moved from location to location, position to position, with no one ever really clarifying certain standards, procedures or expectations for excellence. Everyone has a right to be given a clear picture of excellence.

Be sure all the people in your world and on your team understand your expectations. Clarify the playing field. Ensure employees know:

* The vision and values of the company.
* The company's goals.
* The primary goal of the department.
* The primary goal of the job.
* The sub-goals of the job.
* The standards for excellence.
* The department procedures and policies.

A policy manual is important, but keep it thin! When team members approximate your standards for excellence, be sure to praise them. Offer supportive feedback and encouragement. You will build a winning team.

Moving Into Alignment

Sometimes, even when you've made your expectations clear and outlined procedures, mistakes occur. It is then time for some meaningful correction. You want to put the same care and thought into offering correction as you did outlining your standards of excellence.

Correction is like the wind of resistance geese encounter when they get out of *formation*. Consider if you correct thoughtfully or blow up at the slightest infraction. If the latter is true, you will only further disrupt your team's alignment. Is your harsh criticism preventing your team members from being honest with you about mistakes? Are people covering up when they err? Cover-up will result in your team flying in circles, rather than in *formation*. You will not correct the course quickly and you will waste team energy and effort. You will play a part in creating a demoralized team.

The empowering leader's role is to offer correction in a climate such that everyone commits to continuous improvement and where responsiveness replaces defensiveness. How can you do this? Create an environment in which people know that it's acceptable to say, "I think we've got a problem," instead of waiting for things to blow completely out of proportion. People at every level should feel empowered to say, "Whoops, I think something's not working," instead of waiting for someone else to report the problem. Too often we kill the messenger, the person brave enough to report the problem. Top managers kill the messenger with small comments such as "You know better than that;" "I can't believe you let that happen;" and "What's wrong with you, anyway?"

It's in responding, not reacting, that we cause people to become open, willing to talk about problems, admit problems exist, and enable — at every level in the organization – others to become problem-solvers. When we include people closest to the problem in our pursuit of the solution, we make them more aware of how they can keep problems from occurring. This helps all team members remain open and responsive.

To turn the culture around, make heroes out of the people who report problems, not just the people who solve them. Empower those closest to the problems early in the process versus late in the life cycle. Why wait until you have passed through half a dozen value-added stages to say, "This is wrong. This won't work." Worse yet, why wait for the customer to complain, return a defective item, and demand a credit adjustment or refund?

By empowering your team to stop the process and "shut down the line," you may be amazed at how many errors you begin to eliminate, how much money you save and how you positively impact morale.

Take-Off's

Doug, the superintendent of a general contracting firm, told our Leadership Development LAB about Chris, a young trainee engineer who made a big mistake on a take-off for a set of girders.

"I used his take-off *information* for my job layout," Doug said. "His error ended up costing me over one and a half days of work. Chris was on vacation when I discovered the mistake. When Chris came back to work after his vacation and found out about the error he had made, he came into my office with is tail between his legs, his hat in hand, wondering how I would react. Considering his past experiences with me, I am sure he expected the worst.

Instead of what he was expecting, I said, 'Chris, the mistake you made on the take-off was very similar to one I made several years ago, early in my engineering career.' I went on to tell him my own story of egg on my face. I told him this was a good lesson for all of us and pointed out how important it is that we all double check each other's work. He was relieved that I did not rip his head off. Instead, I helped him save face. I could see his relief helped him open up to my suggestions and feedback. As surprising as it may seem at first, this event, which began with Chris' mistake and me losing a day and a half of productivity, has led to us working together far better than ever. We are a real team.

The lesson I learned from this experience is that I have more power and can be a force for true empowerment when I correct indirectly, and when I help the other person save face instead of ripping off their head.

The action I call you to is to correct with kindness, understanding and patience. Go out of your way to protect the delicate self-esteem of every member of your team. Remembering your own faults and errors will help you to keep the other person's foibles in perspective. If you are courageous enough to admit your faults, you will open up a greater space for honesty and intimacy in all your relationships. The benefit you will gain is loyal, committed employees who are genuine team players. You will find ways to build a team that does repeated practices right the first time, every time, and courageously takes risks to find ways for continuous improvement. You will save time, and helping others save face will help you save money."

Off Course

As Doug's story illustrated, it's a good idea to bear in mind your own errors when correcting others. Many years ago, Jan made a potentially fatal error that he has never forgotten. It helps him maintain perspective when he is called upon to make corrections on his own team. Jan told our Leadership Development LAB:

"In 1969, I was stationed off of the DMZ in the Tonkin Gulf aboard the battleship USS Taylor DD-468. The ship's crew was given orders to stop all fire and support the missions above the 37th parallel DMZ. We were to proceed directly south. This came as a direct order from President Johnson to curtail bombing in North Vietnam. To compound matters, the crew was tired. We had just completed the arduous task of refueling and taking on arms and supplies. All of us had been up for at least 12 hours without a break. My responsibility as a quartermaster was to navigate.

I took over the watch and was given orders by the ship's captain to plot a course of 180 degrees directly south. Whether this was due to fatigue or whatever, I don't know, but I plotted a course of 360 degrees, a complete circle, and had us heading toward Red China. Fortunately, before it was too late, the navigator came to my rescue and slowly but surely, while the captain was sleeping, turned the ship around and headed us south.

The lesson I learned from this experience is to double-check any statements, decisions or actions that not only affect me, but others! I also learned that everyone will and does make mistakes and should be forgiven. People need to be coached, corrected and, on occasion, reprimanded, but not judged.

The action I call you to is to think of your mistakes and blunders before judging others. You will probably think twice and your feedback will become meaningful, supportive and helpful. You will build others instead of creating a team that goes in circles. You will head directly toward your goal. People will come to you for coaching and feedback. Your team will listen to your advice when it is given, and you will reach your goals in the most efficient and effective way."

Start With Praise

Gene, the assistant controller of a large manufacturer, told our Leadership Development Lab about the time he and his supervisors were trying to verify some important financial *information* using a document prepared by one of his staff members. Through this process, he discovered a major discrepancy between his numbers and the document she'd prepared. Since he needed the correct *information* immediately, Gene called her into the meeting to verify the *information* in her document.

"I explained the scope of the project we were involved in," Doug said. "This helped her see how we were using the document. I praised the *information* which matched the source documents. I also pointed out what didn't match up and looked unreasonable. She immediately saw the error she had made and took full ownership and responsibility.

The lesson I learned from this experience is that if I cover the entire project, including what worked when pointing out an error, the person on the receiving end of the correction is far more likely to take responsibility because a portion of their work has generated good results. This puts the error in a context of belief and support. It eliminates the need to be defensive so that solutions can be found and we can move on.

The action I call you to is: point out what was done correctly along with the incorrect items in someone's work. Keep your correction in the context of what has worked. Help the person on the receiving end of the correction keep their self-esteem intact. The benefit you will gain is the person you're correcting will take full responsibility for their actions, and performance will improve."

We can only build a championship team that flies *in formation* by helping all team members accept full responsibility for quality of their work. You cannot make anyone accept responsibility; taking responsibility is a choice. The empowering leader creates an environment where people find it easier to admit errors and accept full responsibility for the outcomes of all of their work. Most of us are past masters at projecting and defensively deflecting, pointing out the errors of others, blaming and shrugging our shoulders. This job of helping your team accept full responsibility is one of the biggest jobs an empowering leader will ever undertake. Keep the challenge in perspective and remember your work will pay off in helping your team, and your organization, grow.

Pain In The Butt

Larry, the purchasing manager for a barge manufacturing company, told our Leadership Development LAB:

"In the 1970s, we were in the midst of a nationwide gasoline shortage. As I look back on those days, I must admit I had made myself the resident 'pain in the butt' to all my co-workers. I constantly and mercilessly teased all my co-workers who ran out of gas, especially if they got stranded. I accused them of only using the top half of their gas tank and gave any other jabs I could think of to hassle or embarrass them about how they were being disadvantaged by the crisis.

Well, as fate would have it, I was out of the office running a lunch-time errand one day, when my car started to cough, sputter, jerk and gasp. The resident 'pain in the butt' had actually run out of gas. I was way out of town and there were no gasoline stations in sight. In fact, I knew there were no gas stations for miles around. For some unexplainable reason, I decided to call the garage at work and I asked that someone quietly bring me a can of gasoline. Unbeknownst to me, they decided to call one of my co-workers and ask him to drive the gas out to me. Well, of course once my fellow employees were alerted to my peril, my worst nightmares happened. I had egg all over my face when I returned to the office. There were signs and banners everywhere announcing that Larry had run out of gas and, of course, an unending source of jibes and comments as to my fate. It was not a pleasant experience.

Later on that evening, I was telling my story to one of my friends. Immediately she said, 'I thought you had AAA road service. Wouldn't AAA have brought you some fuel?' I am sure AAA would have if I had thought to call. Now I had double egg on my face.

The lesson I learned from this experience is to withhold judgment and allow others the same room for error. I learned the absurdity of expecting others to be perfect. This lesson forcefully reminded me of the fact that others will mete out judgment with the same harshness or patience as I mete out judgment on them.

The action I call you to is to lighten up. Remember, the jibes that may feel like joking and fun play to you can feel like stinging, cutting criticism to others. So withhold judgment! The benefit you will gain is living in a more harmonious world, a world which is less harsh. You will experience the empowerment that comes when you know you have the freedom to be yourself. You will experience fewer intensive retributions when you make the inevitable errors we all make."

Discharging

Sometimes, correcting means discharging. Even then, you can follow the traits of an empowering leader to ensure what's best for the team, and the person being discharged. Bob, a production foreman for a ceramics wholesale distributor, told our Leadership Development LAB about having to lay off an associate before the associate returned from his vacation. Bob decided to employ the leadership techniques he had learned, and asked if he could drop by the employee's home to talk.

"Knowing the news that he was being laid off would be upsetting, I decided, in advance, to be an active listener. I knew he might need to vent. When I got there, he asked why he was being laid off. I avoided giving him the kind of critical feedback about his work performance that I could have justified, although I did give a few suggestions about work he might want to try in the future. Still, I didn't want to condemn or complain. I instead told him of a similar experience I had a few years earlier, demonstrating my ability to see things from his point of view.

When I left his house, I could see a faint smile on his face, and I knew he was going to be okay. Three days later, I followed up with the letter of recommendation I had promised, highlighting only this associate's strengths. When I dropped the letter off at a pre-arranged location, I was surprised to find a Thank-You note waiting for me."

Even when you must discharge a team member — you can find something positive, if you try. If you are genuinely interested in the person as a human being and do not criticize, condemn or complain, you assist the person and your team. Always tell the truth about the discharging in non-judgmental terms and offer hope for the future. That will smooth the transition for both of you.

* **Encourage your team to acknowledge mistakes.**

* **Move into alignment by replacing defensiveness with responsiveness.**

* **Begin with praise.**

* **Keep errors in perspective by recalling your own mistakes.**

* **Correct to regroup, even if it means dismissing.**

Five Steps to Problem Solving

State the Pin-Pointed Problem.

Develop and Quantify all Possible Causes.

Develop All Possible Solutions.

Decide on the Best Possible Solution.

Implement the Solution.

>>>15

Practical Problem Solving

The formation of a problem is often more essential than its solution.

Albert Einstein

Fogged In

Alan, a salesperson for a manufactured homes dealership, told our Leadership Development LAB about commuting to and from work in the fog. "On those dark, cool fall mornings, and even sometimes in the evenings, fog can create a very serious, even potentially hazardous, problem. The first thing I did was replace my old, deteriorated windshield wipers. Then I adjusted my high and low beams. The new wipers and adjusted lights helped to some extent in keeping me on my toes and out of trouble. Someone had told me that driving lights with yellow lenses (fog lights) could improve my visibility by 20 to 30 percent. Skeptical, but tired of the struggle, I finally purchased a set of fog lights and soon I had them neatly installed on my '91 Chevrolet pick-up. I eagerly awaited testing them on my next fog-filled drive. Sure enough, a few weeks later I saw a heavy, gray, foggy sky heading my way at about 5:00 p.m., long before I left the office for home. As I pulled out of the parking lot and headed home, I optimistically switched on my new fog lights. To my delight, a soothing ray of yellow pierced the clammy night fog to create a tunnel of clear driving. Since then I have utilized them on numerous occasions and am continually amazed at their ability to pierce the shrouded fog-filled night air so I can see clearly.

This experience taught me that when I am faced with a difficult situation and I can't see my way clearly, it is important for me to try a new idea, ask for and listen to the advice of others who have solved similar problems and move past my natural skepticism. When things seem to be a little foggy for you, try shining a new light on the problem. Try seeing your problem through another lens. You will watch your problems melt away, literally disappear before your very eyes."

The color and quality of our lives is not so much determined by the circumstances, or the shroud of fog in our lives, but rather the lens through which we see our lives. You will find people happy despite difficult circumstances and those who grumble even when fortune has shined on them. Think about your life today. Is there some troubling situation obscuring your vision? Part of your job as an empowering leader is to change the lens and see it differently, and help every member of your team do the same. There are differences in practical problem-solving and complaining. Nothing is good or bad until you label it so. Help those around you change the lens of their lives through your own inspiring positive example.

A Philosophy Of Problem Solving

One of the most important activities that teams engage in is problem solving. Performance teams solve problems when their "scoreboard" indicates that critical areas of performance are below the desired level, the production process is "out of control," quality of work life problems arise in the work area, or they see any opportunity for improvement.

When a team gets together and attempts to solve a problem, they are likely to have difficulty because team members may be using different approaches to solving the problem. Imagine a group of people attempting to dance together, each listening to a different tune. For this reason, it is helpful to agree on a step-by-step process for solving problems. The following illustrates such a philosophy:

Continuous Pursuit of Improvement: Excellence comes through the ardent pursuit of continuous improvement. Becoming world class comes from continuing to set the bar at the next higher level. Satisfaction comes as much from the quest as it does from the accomplishment.

Solve It Now: Problems are best solved as soon as possible. The longer a problem continues, the more the technical system and people begin to adapt to it. Problems solved soon are solved more easily.

No "Other-Guys": Superior problem-solvers have a strong sense of "internal locus of control." This is an acceptance of responsibility, a feeling of control over the events in one's life.

Problems Are Normal: Life is not perfect. Problems occur in every organization. The difference is that in excellent companies people constantly work on solving problems as they occur.

Be Hard on Problems, Easy on People: Avoid blaming others and personalizing the problem. The team should focus on solving the problem, not on whose fault the problem is.

Teams Address the Problems They Can Control: Team members should accept ownership for trying to solve problems in their area of responsibility even if they did not directly cause them.

Problems Are Best Solved By Groups: Two heads (or three or four or more) are better than one if the people involved work well together. A group will have more ideas than one person and be better able to implement a solution.

When Does A Problem Exist?

A problem exists when things are not ideal.

P roblem. What is a problem? A problem is anything that stands between you and continuous improvement in key performance measures.

R ecognize that a problem well stated is a problem half solved! State your problem in a "problematical" statement, not a question. Your well-stated problem will not include the cause of the problem and will not include the solution to your problem. "Pinpoint" the problem, the more specific, the better.

O pen yourself to all possible causes of the problem. Look at every possible option, drop your defensiveness. Give up your ego, your special interest, and your biases about people, methods and procedures.

B e open to all possible solutions. Don't jump to conclusions. Listen, really listen, to every possible solution. Realize that there are at least ten solutions to every problem—two of which are fantastic.

L ook at solutions in the light of resources (time, talent, capital, etc.) to determine the best solution—the one that will best work now.

E xecute — put the solution into action. You must take action, or all the forethought and work will go down the drain as another wasted meeting. Failing to take action when there are infinite possibilities demoralizes what would otherwise be a high-performance team.

M   ake sure the people affected by and/or required to implement the solution are willing to cooperate. Solutions don't work in a vacuum. People implement solutions, and their feelings, fears, interests, and biases must be considered when implementing solutions.

There's a difference between practical problem-solving and throwing up our hands and saying, "We'll have to solve it this way, because that's the way we've always done it," or saying, "Well, you know there's no way to do that." Practical problem-solving is not copying your competitors by throwing money or people at problems. Practical problem-solving is solving our problems within the constraints of limited resources so that our solutions make us more cost-effective. Practical problem-solving is solving problems with creativity and innovation.

All Washed Up

Derra, assistant office manager for a trucking company in Southwest Washington, told our Leadership Development LAB about the time she and her husband Don were sitting in the living room of their home. "We heard a screeching sound coming from the other end of the house. We jumped up, ran down the hall to the utility room and discovered our clothes dryer making the unmistakable grinding, screaming noise of a dry, burned-out bearing. I turned it off in disgust. That night we bemoaned the fact that we would have to buy a new dryer, and we didn't know where the money was going to come from. The next morning I decided to take it apart and fix it myself. I had the make and model number of the machine and location of the bearing written down for my husband before he got up. I asked Don, who works in Portland, to pick up the bearing we needed during his lunch hour. He said it was ridiculous for me to try to fix it, and was upset that I had gone ahead and taken it apart. He wanted us to just bite the bullet and buy a new dryer. I told him, "The parts will be far less than a new dryer, trust me on this; and please pick up the bearing for me."

That night he brought the parts home, still complaining about how crazy I was trying to fix the dryer, and how pointless the whole thing was. I told him not to worry, I was going to fix it. Although it took a little longer than I anticipated, by midnight I had it all back together. It was quieter than a new one, at least to me.

The lesson I learned from this experience is the importance of listening to my own inner voice, the importance of trusting myself no matter what, or how loudly, the nay-sayers speak. As long as I really believe I can do something, I must act bravely and continue moving forward, one step at a time.

Here are the steps I followed:

Step 1. Define the problem (Example: Listen to source and kind of noise).

Step 2. Think ahead and develop a plan. (Example: Carefully disassemble, labeling parts with masking tape as you go, so re-assembly will go more quickly and easily.)

Step 3. Empower support team. (Example: Write down part numbers with complete *information* in detail so correct parts will be procured the first time.)

Step 4. Re-assemble as soon as possible while the memory of the process is fresh in mind.

When you are faced with a problem, follow the four problem steps, explore for cause, look at all your options, believe in yourself. Take the most expedient, cost effective action without fear or trepidation. Don't allow the negative remarks of others to slow you down. Be your own cheerleader. The benefit you will gain is a life full of achievement and success, and as a result you will have truly earned confidence in yourself. You will never feel all washed up."

When you encounter obstacles, problems and barriers, dissolve them, don't solve them. When you discover their cause, they work with you, not against you, to improve your organization and your thinking.

Problem Solving Wheel

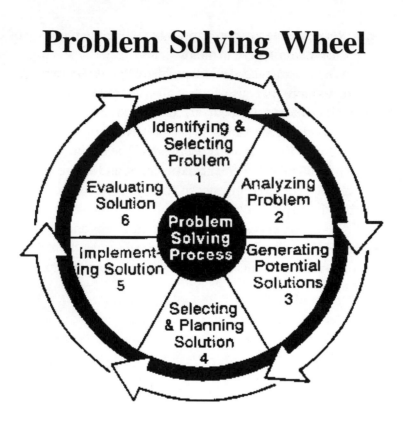

Tips On Defining The Problem

The most important aspect of defining a problem is to state it in a way for everyone to have the same understanding so that the group will know what to look for in a solution. Without a specific, pinpointed definition, each team member will assume his or her own definition. Each member may then be working to solve a different problem than the other team members. If you can clearly state your problem and put it in the sunlight, you can solve that problem. Ask yourself many times, and make yourself answer, "Just what is the problem?"

Everyone must agree on the problem:
1. Clarify wording. Be specific.
2. Ask questions of each other (gain knowledge through teamwork).
3. Ask questions of the process (gain knowledge from process data).

Diagrams For Problem-Solving

Consider Pareto Diagrams and Fishbone Diagrams:

Pareto Diagrams

   Vilfredo Pareto was an Italian economist who defined the 80/20 rule. He said that 80 percent of the problem comes from 20 percent of the activities. When the 20 percent that is causing 80 percent of the trouble is identified, the team can make better use of their time.

   A Pareto diagram is a bar chart used to determine which cause to work on first to improve the process. The causes are listed on the X axis (horizontal). The frequency or cost associated with each problem is plotted on the Y axis (vertical). The Pareto diagram allows us to determine what the major problems are, i.e., those that happen with the greatest frequency. The Pareto diagram allows us to separate the "vital few" from the "trivial many."

Steps in Making a Pareto Diagram
1. Define the problem.
2. Brainstorm causes and select the ones to use on the diagram.
3. Select the time period to be covered.
4. Collect data using a check sheet and total the frequency of occurrence for each cause during the time period.
5. Draw the X and Y axis putting the proper unit on the Y axis.

6. Under the X axis, write in the most important causes (greatest frequency) first, then the next most important, etc.
7. Draw in the bars. The height of the bar will correspond to the value on the vertical axis.
8. Title the graph and include other important *information*.

A Pareto diagram is one of the first steps in making improvements to a process. It points out the major causes of problems and provides a method of obtaining consensus of opinion on what the major problems are. It helps you to concentrate limited resources on key areas.

It is important to use common sense when you interpret Pareto diagrams. For example, a Pareto diagram on types of injuries does not take into account the severity of the injuries. Hand cuts may have the greatest frequency, but you may want to work on eye injuries first.

Fishbone Diagrams

A Fishbone diagram is used to identify possible causes responsible for the problem at a particular point in time. Construction of a fishbone chart does not solve a problem, but ensures that we do not easily overlook a cause or apply fixes where they are unnecessary.

The causes originate in:
* Materials
* Methods
* Measurement
* Machines
* People
* Environment

The advantages of using a fishbone diagram include decreasing the chance that something is overlooked, and our attention is concentrated on causes.

The disadvantages are that the diagram does not say what the larger sources of variation are, that the cure is not necessarily known if only a cause is shown.

Getting Help

When we updated our main computer system at Turbo Management Systems for our office manager, we ran into a few problems. We bought a new monitor, which was deeper than the former model, so large, in fact, that we could no longer fit the keyboard and the monitor on the desk return. Our solution was to place the computer and the keyboard on the desk itself. That was a little high to be comfortable and made it difficult for our office manager to greet customers and friends coming into the office. We replaced the return with a wider one, but this created more of a problem, including her not being able to open her center drawer. Finally, we brainstormed some possible solutions to the problem, such as a rearview mirror for the office manager to be able to see people as they were coming and going without having to turn around. We also came up with the idea to possibly have some kind of a pull-out return for the keyboard. I decided to go see my friend Ken at an office supply store.

When I told Ken our problem, he said, "Let me see. Here's a monitor stand with a pull-out keyboard carrier combined. Would that work?" Perfect! It was only $65 and took only three minutes to install!

The lesson I learned is that when I have a problem, I should be open to all possible solutions and advice rather than live with inefficiencies. Most importantly, I should seek the advice of experts who know more about how to solve a particular problem than I would. We spent hours trying to resolve a situation Ken handled in minutes. Look around for any problems or headaches. I'll bet you have one or two. Brainstorm for all possible solutions. Ask experts for help and advice. The benefit you gain is a tremendous sense of victory for having solved a nagging problem.

* Help those around you change the lens of
their lives.

* Clearly define the problem.

* Adapt a philosophy of problem solving.

* Use problem analysis tools.

* Seek help from the outside when needed.

Meetings

We met in the morning.
Presumably for problem sorting.
What problem, I wasn't sure
It wasn't defined.
Most of the people just seemed to whine.
We met at 8:00.
Almost everyone was late.
We met at 9:00
I am not sure why, everything seemed fine.
We met at 10:00,
What again? A message to send.
It was down from above
> *Without much love*
We met at 11:00 all four of us...
Sue, Mark, George, and Kevin.
We met again at noon
Brown bags.
The presenter looked like a buffoon.
We met at 1:00, not much fun.
We met at 2:00. I hope we are through.
We met at 3:00, looked at a problem-solving tree.
We met at 4:00. Oh yes, one more.
We met at 5:00.
Everyone was barely alive.
We really took a dive.
Let's start over in the morning
And begin with problem sorting.

-Larry W. Dennis, Sr.

>>>16

Meaningful Meetings

It usually takes more than three weeks to prepare a good impromptu speech.

Mark Twain

Ken has been the distribution center manager of a regional mass merchandising company for over two decades. He said that since Turbo Management's training, he feels as if he is working for an entirely different organization than the one where he began his career. He said, "As an example, over my whole career, I've always hated attending meetings. They have been such a waste of time. Now, I'm showing up at meetings to which I'm not even invited."

It is a fact that most of us have attended far more nonproductive meetings than productive meetings. One of the best strategies you can use as an empowering leader is to plan and facilitate effective meetings.

The performance team must have effective ways to communicate if it is to keep up with all of the *information* and changes that occur in our fast-changing world. If used correctly, meetings can be a great way to keep the performance team informed, up-to-date, and build relationships. Poorly planned meetings waste time and effort and pull your team out of alignment.

Stumbling Blocks

Meetings are often used very casually. In many cases, there is only a vague notion about the objective of a the meeting, and quite often objectives are mixed.

Meetings can be used to solve problems, plan, and help make decisions. Creativity is a vital component of such meetings because it develops alternatives, enriches possibilities, and improves project consequences. There is evidence that managers habitually, maybe unknowingly, discourage creativity and free speculation.

Managers often use their power unwisely. Rank can be used and it is accepted practice for the manager to exercise power and the other members to play it. The consequences are that their prejudices can inhibit the open proposal of alternatives and new ideas.

In almost any meeting, there is a high level of antagonism toward new ideas. When ideas are subjected to immediate criticism, their value and potential are easily destroyed. New ideas are at least worth exploring, since they suggest possibilities for alternative paths, but the negative reflex one customarily observes against a new idea foreshortens their possibilities. The negative reflex also has a further effect; the person who has advanced a new idea or suggestion is a human being and as such identifies with their own suggestion. We perceive a negative reflex response as a personal put-down.

Creativity can provide us with valuable new ideas and perspective. Like any critical resource, we can nurture and protect it by learning to accept the creativity as not something that we learn, but as something we've forgotten that can be relearned. View the stimulation of creativity as a vital part of the team, regardless of job or role definition. Focus upon the idea generation without judgment; analysis can come later. Support and build your own creative ideas from all team members at whatever stage those ideas appear. Remember that being creative is an act of personal faith in our ability to effect positive changes in ourselves, our teams, and our organizations.

There are other stumbling blocks built in the traditional meeting which the careful and conscientious leader can reduce or eliminate. Your first step must be to recognize subtle destruction when it occurs.

Cheryl, a manufacturing service supervisor for a dental equipment manufacturer, told our Leadership Development LAB: "I have a department meeting every month in the dental furniture conference room. Each month, I publish the agenda that I want to cover and ask our department members to add their input. The meeting is attended primarily by our own department and occasionally we invite outside guests. Each month I show graphs of our department's performance for vendor on-time delivery, quality, cycle count accuracy, purchase money, actual vs. planned, relative to productive hours, etc.

Every month, I would present the *information*, explain everything pertinent and then ask if anyone had questions or wanted to offer additional input. After we completed this task, each person would bring up their areas of concern. We would discuss their concerns and try to resolve those issues.

After using this same meeting format for several years, I decided this fall that we needed a change to stimulate new ideas, expand our employees' comfort zones and add additional *information* to our meeting format. All the people in my department have their own computer so I knew this would be an opportunity for them to really expand their horizons by utilizing many of the computer classes we had just completed.

I needed to make a presentation on forklift safety. I decided to ask my receiving clerk, Pat, to make the presentation since he is the most knowledgeable. Pat showed the new overheads on forklift safety as well as adding additional safety tips and *information* that he felt was important. I could easily see his pride as he ran the meeting. This was an opportunity for him to show off his skills in front of the rest of the department, present his own views as well as adding additional *information*.

The lesson I learned from this experience is the importance of waking up and recognizing the many talents of my team. I learned that I can easily allow myself to get boxed in.

The action I call you to is rethink your team meetings and the talents of each of your team members and allow them to expand their horizons. It is amazing what you will learn, and you may be able to far better utilize and capitalize on your team's talents on a daily basis. You will stimulate their creativity, and they will grow to their fullest potential."

Planning the Environment

Increase your chances of a successful meeting by planning and designing the physical environment so that it is conducive to listening and concentrating on the topics being discussed.

Some guidelines for choosing your meeting location:

A designated room. Consistency is helpful and having one room that the performance team always meets in will help. If meetings are consistently held in the same place, attendance and timeliness will occur much more quickly.

Find a room with minimal distractions. If your work area is in a production environment with operating equipment, you will want to find a meeting room that avoids these distracting noises.

No interruptions. If necessary, put a 'Do Not Disturb, Meeting in Progress' sign on the door of the meeting room. It should be agreed upon that others will not interrupt meetings unless there is a genuine emergency.

Set the room up for comfort. Have good lighting, minimal noise and comfortable seating so that team meetings can be as pleasant as possible for everyone concerned.

Arrange the room. The seating arrangements will have a significant impact on team members' behavior. The definition of roles and responsibilities in a team meeting are very different from the classroom, and the arrangement of tables and chairs should reflect the difference. The leader or facilitator of the meeting is not teaching or controlling the meeting. The leader or facilitator should not be the dominant personality or speaker. The leader's job is to encourage team members to participate. The seating arrangements should signify equal participation and responsibility. Avoid having the leader sit or stand on a higher platform, behind a desk or in any way appear to be the 'teacher'.

Planning Effective Meetings

Grant, a veterinarian, told our Leadership Development Lab the following:

"When I entered into hospital merger talks with three other veterinarians last Wednesday, I was ready. I had promised the others that I would have a merger activities timeline ready for their review, and I did. I produced a document, four pages in length, consisting of four columns per page. In the first column, I detailed the many tasks necessary to be completed prior to our merger. The other three columns were left blank, their function to be determined by a discussion among our members. By consensus we decided that the second column would contain the name of the person assigned to each task listed in the first column. The deadline for the task to be completed was put into the third column, and column four would list the actual completion date.

I had also been asked to have some sketches ready of possible floor plans for our planned addition to the central hospital. My new partners were expecting me to show them penciled drawings. Instead I produced four alternative floor plans which I had created on my computer program and printed on my laser printer. Everyone at the meeting was astounded at the detail of these early plans. We spent more than an hour going over the plans, making changes and improvements and dreaming of how our new hospital would operate. No one seemed to expect so much detail and obvious preparation on my part.

My preparation allowed me to move the course of the meeting in the direction we needed it to go. That's not to say I completely dominated the discussion. In fact, I encouraged others to sound out their ideas. However, when those ideas led away from productive discourse, I was able to bring us back around to the important issues.

The lesson I learned is that my confidence grows immensely when I visualize ahead of time what is likely to take place in a meeting and successfully anticipate all the needs of my audience. When I plan all the alternatives and am well prepared, I have options available which I have already considered. By being prepared, I am seldom unsettled by the unexpected. My preparation allows me to take charge of the situation to lead because I better understand the issues at hand. I learned once again that preparation is the great secret to success in whatever I do.

The action I call you to is to take the extra time needed up front to be fully prepared. Take charge and prepare the agenda and take all the time you need to be prepared and feel confident and in control of the situation.

The benefit you will gain from your extra up-front effort is that you will be in command and you will consolidate the team for maximum results."

There are four major steps for planning your effective team meetings:

1. **Determine the purpose.** Meeting for the sake of meeting is a big waste of time. Set a goal or purpose for each meeting. Some performance teams have daily meetings to discuss production work schedules, parts inventories and maintenance work and scheduling. These meetings have a purpose. Other meetings have the goal of solving specific problems or discussing current issues that impact the performance team.

2. **Decide the length of the meeting.** Performance team meetings normally run thirty minutes to an hour, but should never last more than two hours. Deciding beforehand the length of a meeting helps to keep the meeting moving. The number of

people in the meeting, the difficulty of the topic, the number of topics and the group's work schedule are all factors to consider when setting the meeting length. Remember to stick to the meeting schedule! A meeting that goes past its finishing time will lose the interest of the team. Keep in mind the production work schedules or store hours.

3. **Inform participants.** An agenda is the best way to let others know the purpose of the meeting. Along with the purpose, you should include the time of the meeting, where it will be held and if it is necessary to bring or study anything before the meeting begins. If support people who are not regular members attend the meeting, then spend some extra time explaining the topic and what you expect them to contribute.

4. **Choose a facilitator.** Often it helps to have a person at the meeting who is only concerned with keeping to the agenda and the time frame of the meeting. This person will make sure that everyone is heard and that the group stays on the topic until a decision is reached.

Team Meeting Preparation Checklist:

Use the following checklist to be sure you have not forgotten anything for your team meeting:

_____ 1. Have you planned what the team should accomplish at the meeting?

_____ 2. Have you decided what type of activities the team is going to do during the meeting to accomplish your objectives?

_____ 3. Have you planned what you are going to do if you do not get a response from your team? Do you have any questions or suggestions to increase team member participation?

_____ 4. Do you have a written agenda?

_____ 5. Has the agenda been circulated in advance of the meeting?

_____ 6. Have the agenda topics been prioritized?

_____ 7. Have time limits been set for each agenda item?

_____ 8. Did you allow participants to add items to the agenda?

_____ 9. Do you have the necessary *information* collected for the meeting? Do team members know what *information* they should bring with them?

_____10. Have you invited all the necessary people?

_____11. Have you selected a meeting time? Can everyone on your team meet at this time?

_____12. Is there an appropriate space set aside to conduct the meeting with a "do not disturb" order issued for the duration of the meeting?

_____13. Does everyone on your team know when, where, and how long the meeting will last?

Brainstorm Success

Dave, a warehouse supervisor for a dental equipment manufacturer, told our Leadership Development LAB:

"The warehouse staff and I got together and had a brainstorming session. I had been supervising the warehouse for eight months and was scheduled to change positions in the company on the first of the following month. Before leaving this position, I decided we should have a meeting to brainstorm some of the many achievements the warehouse had accomplished during my management. This was not our usual brainstorming session of looking for answers to troublesome problems.

With a flip chart titled 'Warehouse 1995 Achievements' and a volunteer scribe, we set our stopwatch for five minutes and got ready to begin brainstorming. Before starting, I explained that any achievement, no matter how large or small, should be mentioned and listed on the chart. I said, 'We want to list as many items as we possibly can in just five minutes.'

The list of achievements came very slow at first, since many of our achievements weren't that visual. Once the people in our group got going and saw that it was okay to list even the smallest things, we broke open like a gusher and the long list of achievements we had been involved in sprung out. We ended up going for 10 minutes and filling up two full flip chart pages. When we were finished and had read through our list of achievements, we found that in eight short months we had accomplished a great deal together, far more than we ever realized.

There was a sense of joy and accomplishment in the air. I could feel it as it swept over the room. The atmosphere was different. We were operating on a higher plane. As the team members looked at each other it was with an even greater sense of pride and fulfillment, and this change in the atmosphere happened in 10 short minutes. Wow!

The lesson I learned from this experience is that brainstorming is a powerful way not only to solve problems, but to help the team look at their achievements and successes. I also learned that looking at achievements through brainstorming truly does turbo-charge the atmosphere.

The action I call you to is take the time - 10 minutes - to use the tool of brainstorming with your team and look back over your collective shoulders at your achievements and successes for the past year. Through this process, you will experience the power of positive, reflective thinking. This will help you blast through any resistance to continued improvement you may be experiencing.

The benefit you and your team will gain is a sense of what has been accomplished, and it will revive you and your team to take on more, and bigger, challenges."

Starting Your Meeting

Plan to begin all your meetings in an upbeat way. The way I have used for years in our Monday team meetings is to have everyone tell the highlight of their weekend. Time these highlights. We keep ours to about 45 seconds per person. It keeps team members tuned in on one another's personal lives and values, builds community, deepens understanding and is a way to express interest in one another. It is a way to get participation from everyone before addressing the more serious matters at hand.

You might also kick-off with an inspirational quote and then move into the meeting itself with the performance team celebrating the successes of the former week. If you have guests, it is important they are introduced. We always include them in our initial warm-up, even if they are outside vendors or perspective team members.

Introduce the agenda and the purpose of the meeting. Then explain what decisions have to be made, what results are expected from the meeting and the time that is available. If the agenda is not full, ask for additional agenda topics from the group. If the agenda is full, begin discussion of the topics as soon as possible after you kick-off the meeting. It is very easy to begin talking about other related topics, especially if the scheduled ones are unpleasant. It is the meeting facilitator's job to ensure the group doesn't move too far adrift. Simply say: "This is very interesting and we need to get back to the agenda," or "Let's take this up at another time so we can finish on schedule." The facilitator politely brings the discussion back on target. It is a good idea to leave the agenda on a flip chart out in full view, pointing to it while reminding the group what they were there to talk about. Other agenda topics can be written down on the flip chart to be dealt with at another meeting.

Everyone at the meeting has a valuable opinion and should be encouraged to express it; however, sometimes talkative people tend to take up the whole meeting time. The facilitator's job is to make sure everyone gets an opportunity to speak. This can be done by asking people directly, such as "Hey Jim, what do you think we should do?" You can gently coach people who are doing most of the talking by saying, "I believe we understand your opinion, Al. Let's see what Sally has to say about this."

At the beginning of the meeting, assign a person to take notes. Ask that person to pay special attention to all decisions that are made. At the end of the meeting, have that person review all of the decisions to ensure all the meeting members agree and that the agreement to act has been accepted. Ask if any support is necessary from others at the meeting to complete agreed-upon actions. Have all people present state the action to which they have now committed.

After reviewing the actions, it is time to review the agenda to check that all meeting goals have been accomplished. If not, set another meeting time while the team is still in the room. Ask if there is anything else that needs to be brought up or if additional discussion is necessary. If all agenda items have not been met, then decide what should be done. The group may decide to continue the meeting or schedule one for another time. Thank everyone for participating and conclude the meeting on time!

Meetings are a terrific way to keep the team in alignment, thus obtaining that 71 percent advantage. Meetings move people forward. During a successful meeting, the following occurs:

1. **Performance is reviewed.** Performance teams do not just focus on problems, they manage performance. The team's Subject Area Expert (SAE) will presents the team's performance data. (The SAE reports on such things as percentage of fulfilled orders, scrap rates, production rates, average ticket size, number of failed welds and average tons per day.) The presentation includes the team's current levels of performance versus its goals, recent trends in the data and any variations in the performance data.

2. **Success is recognized.** It is every person's job to be sure that extra effort and improvements in performance are celebrated. We all enjoy recognition for a job well done. The team leader or any other member of the team can show appreciation for contributions to the team's performance. Providing recognition increases the likelihood that the performance will continue to improve. So don't forget those honks of encouragement.

3. **Problems are solved.** A structured problem-solving process is used to attack problems and develop solutions.
4. **Next steps are planned.** Following the review of team performance, the team plans what steps members must take next. If the team has experienced good performance, team members discuss how to maintain that level of empowering performance. If the team's performance is poor, action steps are determined for correcting the poor performance.
5. **News and *information* is shared.** Performance team meetings can also be used to share general business *information* that would otherwise not be shared at all or shared in other meetings.
6. **Communication and coordination takes place.** Performance teams interact as needed with other teams to accomplish goals. Team members may visit other team meetings to ensure cooperation and coordinated action.

Develop A Code Of Conduct

Productive behavior in meetings does not just happen; it must be created. A strong prompt for getting desirable behavior in a meeting is a code of conduct. This is a list of "meeting rules" or guidelines for appropriate meeting behavior. The list can be hung in the meeting room, reviewed at the beginning of the meeting and referred to when/if inappropriate behavior occurs.

Why should we develop a code of conduct?

1. To create common expectations and understanding among team members.
2. To gain commitment from individual team members to constructive behavior.
3. To enhance the self-management of the team.

The group will be more committed to conforming to the code if people work as a group to establish that code. You may find it helpful to provide a "sample" Code of Conduct as a model, such as the following:

1. Stick to the topic at hand. If you have other issues to discuss, wait until the one being discussed is resolved.
2. Make criticism constructive. Avoid value judgments and try to suggest alternatives.
3. Arrive on time and end on time.
4. Pay attention to whomever is speaking. Be a good listener.
5. Respect each other. One person talks at a time.
6. No gossip! Keep discussions on issues over which the group has control.
7. Contribute. Everyone has the responsibility to bring something to the meeting.
8. Share ideas. Ideas belong to the group, not the individual.
9. Remember that what is said here, stays here: confidentiality.
10. Leave your stripes at the door.

11. Be frank and honest. Keep an open mind.
12. Appreciate when something good happens, and say so.
13. Leave united. The team speaks with one voice after a decision is made.

Meetings Matter

Stewart, store manager for a major Northwest mass merchandiser, told our Leadership Development LAB:

"I committed over a year ago to have monthly all-store employee meetings. In this way I would have contact with every employee at least once per month. The meetings are needed for inspiration, motivation, training and setting direction for our store. I hadn't been doing this consistently and had been feeling guilty. I knew I had committed to conducting the meeting, I just couldn't seem to get around to it. I knew it was important, but I just didn't have time.

When we started talking about putting more enthusiasm into our work, I knew immediately this is where I needed to apply the extra commitment, follow through and determination. The very next day I told my training specialist to just schedule the meetings and I would be there regardless of what I was doing.

I am now in my second round of meetings and the results are amazing. I am finding out about many things our team didn't know, and I am getting some great ideas from them on how to increase sales and customer service. Our employees are very happy that I am just taking some time to talk with them. The 20 minutes I had anticipated these meetings would take has quickly become an hour — the best hour of our week! At one meeting in particular, I took a chance and shared some thoughts of a personal nature, feeling a little uncomfortable for doing so, and not quite sure what the response might be. I was rewarded with a warm and caring response from the whole team, and I sensed a deeper relationship with each team member.

The lesson I have learned from this experience is that when I take the risk, make the commitment, set aside time with my team and am open and honest, I can really improve my relationship with my team.

The action I call you to is have more and better meetings with your team and, when you do, take the risk of opening up and being more vulnerable. Let the real you show through. Be open and honest with your people. The benefit you will gain is a better and deeper relationship with your team. You will improve productivity, reduce turnover and increase sales, service and profits."

Turbo Management Systems urges all its clients to conduct more, better, shorter meetings; those with a clear purpose and agenda, meetings that start and end on time; and meetings where action items are reported on and new commitments are made. We encourage you to conduct meetings that excite, empower and motivate your team to peak performance!

Speaking Before Groups

An important part of your skill set as an empowering leader is your ability to express yourself confidently and competently in front of both large and small groups. This may occur at a meeting or you may find yourself literally on-stage. To be more confident in front of a group, know your subject. The more you know about a subject, the more confident you will be. Researching and studying the subject can certainly help build confidence. However, the greatest single builder of confidence comes from the experience you have had in the laboratory of your own life.

Develop Confidence and Competence in Front of Groups

Call it evaluation anxiety or stage fright, performance anxiety or Richard Nixon disease (understandable to those who viewed his disastrous, sweaty-lipped 1960 Presidential debate with John Kennedy). The fear of speaking in public is dreaded like no other dread. "Study after study indicates that public speaking is our most common fear — ranking even above death," says Jerilyn Ross, president of Phobia Society of America. "And it's one of the few fears that affects men and women equally; most phobias affect women twice as often as men, but not public speaking."

This is a fear that knows no sex or age barriers one that sends butterflies fluttering in the stomachs of as many as 80 percent of the population, according to some psychologists. Those butterflies turn into all-out phobic fear, "resulting in heart palpitations, shortness of breath, shaky hands, weak knees and a feeling of impending doom, in as many as five percent of the U.S. population," says Ross.

If you're among the sweaty-palmed masses, you're in good company. Sir Laurence Oliver, Mr. Thespian himself, is said to have been tormented by stage fright for six years. Jovial Willard Scott reportedly isn't so jolly right before showtime. He says he fights the jitters every morning. Even Fidel Castro, well known for his ever present hand-rolled smokes, admits to having a fear of public speaking.

"The reason most people fear public speaking is it makes them feel so vulnerable," says Ross. "We're up there and sense we're being judged. And that brings out all our fears of how people see us, how we look, how we sound and how we relate to people. When we're speaking in public we feel like we're on display and being evaluated."

The secret of confidence in making a presentation in front of a group is learning to analyze and think through your experience before you present it to your audience. Analyze the experience in terms of: What happened? When did it happen? Where did it happen? Who was involved?

When we learn to analyze our experiences, we can draw reasonable conclusions as to why things happen. In making presentations in front of a group, which is outside the comfort zone of the average adult, it is wise to begin with realistic subjects. Realistic subjects would certainly be those experiences through which we have lived. In other words, talk about you. Whenever we stray away from our own experience, give an opinion or speak in generalities, we lose credibility with our audience. What better topic than an experience you have lived through? Choose anecdotes that you might have excitedly told a friend or family member, stories with punch and a point.

Those who are willing to take the microphone in hand, walk to the platform and address the audience are driven to make a difference in the world. There is passion in the vision that every individual can become happier, more successful and achieve dreams. But is passion enough? What can compel an individual in the audience to risk, have enough courage where a moment ago there was none, and take action changing the destiny of their life? A speaker who can inspire such action is truly skilled in the most sophisticated of crafts, yet the rules for such presentations are very SIMPLE:

S **ubject.** Talk about an experience from the lab of your life, a subject you cannot forget, that has meaning for and to you.

I **llustrations** and examples. Make your presentation come alive. Be specific (dates, time, place) and describe things clearly (color, size, shape, temperature).

M **ake** an outline. When did it happen? Where did it happen? Who was involved? What happened?

P **lan** your presentation. Do not write your presentation word for word. Do not try to memorize it. Think it through by following the When, Where, Who, What, Why outline. Talk your presentation out with a friend.

L **et** yourself have fun. Do not worry about your delivery. Use your voice and body fully. If you have fun, really have fun, your delivery will take care of itself.

E **nvision** yourself. See yourself in your mind's eye having a successful experience before the presentation is made. Use your imagination. See the smiles on the faces of your audience. See them leaning forward attentively. Hear the laughter. Hear the applause as your presentation is completed. Hear the favorable comments that follow your presentation. Feel the firm grasp of congratulatory handshakes. Feel how good it is to do a great job and know it. Experience your success in your mind as all champions do before they experience their success in reality.

Following are some helpful tools for developing and holding meaninful meetings.

STANDARD TEAM MEETING AGENDA

I.   Review Agenda (Time Frame:____minutes)

II.   Recognition of Team members (Time Frame:____minutes)

III. *Who should be recognized for positive achievement?*

IV. *Information* Sharing (Time Frame:____minutes)

V.   *What needs to be shared (technical information, news, items from senior teams, etc.)*

VI. Performance review (Time Frame:____minutes)

VII. *Objectively review team performance measures. Set goals. Discuss the team's performance with respect to the goals.*

VIII. Review Existing Action Items (Time Frame:____minutes)

IX. Problem Solving (Time Frame:____minutes)

X.   *Which problem or performance will you try to solve or improve?*

XI. *Choose one or two of the following problem-solving steps for the meeting:*

     1.   *Define the Problem*

     2.   *Brainstorm Causes*

     3.   *Analyze Data*

     4.   *Brainstorm Solutions*

     5.   *Reach Consensus*

     6.   *Develop Action Plan*

XII. Action Planning (Time Frame:____minutes)

XIII. *What needs to be done before the next meeting?*

XIV. *Complete the "Team Action Plan" (or the Action Agreement Register)*

XV. Plan Next Team Meeting Agenda (Time Frame:____minutes)

Team Name _____ Date _____

Team Leader Name_____

Action Agreement Register

Who? (Name)	Is Going to do What?	By When?	Completed?

Participants Records

Agreement Record for_____

Date	Agreement	Due Date/Time	Kept On Time	Revoked or Remade	Missed

* Avoid meeting stumbling blocks.

* Plan meeting environment.

* Prepare for the meeting.

* Stick to the agenda.

* Have a code of conduct.

Listen

Listen -
I am
Listen -
I Will
Listen -
In a Minute
Listen -
Be Still
Listen - To what I say,
    Don't hold me at bay.
Listen - Don't agree,
    Just listen to me.
Listen - Can't you see?
    I'm not sure of me.
Listen.

    -Larry W. Dennis, Sr.

>>>17

Listening Leader

People ask the difference between a leader and a boss. The leader works in the open, and the boss in the covert. The leader leads, and the boss drives.

Theodore Roosevelt

Go Fish

Andrew, a salesperson for a steel distribution center, came home from work exhausted. He was tired and grouchy. It was 6 p.m. and he was facing a mountain of paperwork and a stack of dishes in the kitchen sink. His 'to do' list had grown impossibly long. His 6-year-old daughter, Camber, asked him to play. He immediately dropped everything, and father and daughter took up a game of Go Fish.

"As we played cards, I asked about her day. She told me about her friend next door and the friend's new kitten," Andrew said. "I asked her, 'What was the best thing that happened to you at school today?' As she talked, I really listened.

After about 30 minutes, she spontaneously jumped up, ran around the table and gave her father a big hug.

"Daddy, I love you," she said.

"I love you, too," he answered.

Then she said, "Do you know why I love you?"

"Why sweetheart?"

"Because," she said, "You listen to me."

"Wow!" thought Andrew. "I didn't get that much of a response after we got her a bike at Christmas or the birthday party at Chuck E. Cheese." He said he couldn't remember a time when his daughter had ever been more spontaneous expressing her love.

"The lesson I learned from this experience is that when I listen, really listen, to others, when I reward them with my attentiveness, they reward me with a feeling of joy beyond explanation. I learned that nothing on my 'to do' list is so important that I can't take time out to listen to those I love."   Pay attention to the important people in your life - your friends, family and your team. When you listen to others, you provide a form of compensation that is far more valuable than a 10 percent raise. That doesn't mean we must agree and it doesn't mean we have to compromise our values; we simply genuinely listen and respect the other person's point of view.

Listening is the number-one way to better understand the unique personalities of every team member. Communication is more than merely sending a message. Good communicators are competent receivers. Listening is at least fifty percent of all effective communications. Think about your best friends. You may have chosen them, in part, because they know how to listen to your concerns.

Recent research shows we feel most acknowledged when:

* others listen to us,
* we receive praise,
* we are touched appropriately,
* we receive positive feedback,
* our boundaries are respected, and
* our agreements with others are maintained.

To build a championship team, we must be willing to listen to one another. As an empowering leader, find a way to show your respect and honor of others by listening to those on your team.

Effective listening skills are as important for an empowering leader to develop as effective speaking skills. Most people seem to feel they listen well. The worst listeners, unfortunately, are often the biggest talkers. We were born with one tongue and two ears. Empowering leaders use them proportionately.

Slip Sliding Away

Glen, the superintendent of a bridge construction company, told our Leadership Development LAB about a crane operator who walked off a job-site without saying a word.

"I called the subcontractor's project manager to ask why the crane operator had walked off. He said the ground was cracking alongside the tracks of the crane and the operator was afraid it would cave in and tip the crane over into the footings that were 20-feet deep. They wanted to get a larger crane with a longer reach so they could sit back farther from the hole.

It was easy enough to see the crane operator's point. Still, that didn't justify his walking off the job-site. The problem was it would take at least a week to get the larger crane with a longer reach. This would, in effect, bring the entire project to a halt, throw the project behind schedule, prolong public inconvenience and drive up costs. I asked the project manager and crane operator to meet me at the job-site the next morning. I decided to listen to their concerns and see if they had any ideas for getting the job done on schedule.

As we walked over to the site, I carefully explained the inconveniences and all the costs of delaying the project. I wanted the two to understand their role in the big picture and the importance of their contributions. And then I listened. They appreciated that instead of my just blasting them, I presented my concerns without doing all the talking. As I listened to them, they came up with an idea. They told me of an encounter with a similar problem on another site. As we continued walking and they continued talking, they became convinced that they should let us excavate the area that was cracking — a space about 40-feet long, 8-feet wide and 6-feet deep. They would stack crane mats as backup and reinforcement. They then would carefully walk their crane out over the mats. We went into action. Our crews did the excavation. They brought in the crane mats. We only lost two days instead of a week or more. The project remained on schedule. The lesson I learned is the importance of keeping the lines of communication open."

Glen could have berated the crane operator and his boss for walking off the job. Instead, he listened to their concerns, and provided them enough background about the project that they felt empowered to suggest improvements. By listening, and letting the people closest to the actual work propose solutions, Glen saved his project.

Deliberately orchestrate opportunities to get together with all your team members, the subs, the inspectors, your own crew and all the important people back at your office. Get to know everyone you possibly can. Make specific plans to contact everyone you can on your team.

Why not conduct an "Inner-View" with at least one team member this week? What is an "Inner-View?" It is an informal meeting — often done over a cup of coffee – where you ask questions about the person's history, interests, and concerns. Listen. The next time you run into that team member, be sure to ask about something you were told, such as the sick parent or the bowling tournament. The benefits you will gain by conducting the "Inner-View" and getting to really know your team are greater understanding and renewed enthusiastic relationships. You will not be caught by people walking off your job or displaying attitudes of resignation. Instead, you will have a team of committed problem-solvers.

Consider these goals as an effective listener:

1. To express an attitude of genuine interest, acceptance and understanding.
2. To encourage the expression of the other person's idea.
3. To strengthen relationships.
4. To increase readiness to accept change.
5. To develop teamwork.
6. To improve morale.
7. To broaden our knowledge.
8. To improve the quality of the team's decisions.

Make Time To Listen

Dave, a warehouse supervisor for a dental equipment manufacturer, told our Leadership Development LAB about promoting a team member. "Jack was excellent at all the operational aspects of the warehouse; in spite of this, the operation didn't run with the precision I know is possible," Dave said. "He needed to improve his personal relationships with the other warehouse staff. I tried to explain to Jack that by improving his relationships he would set up an environment that would breed ideas for improvement and people would want to work with him as a team.

In spite of what I thought was a great explanation, it didn't appear to me that Jack was making a lot of progress. Then I had a flash. I decided I should lead by example and start by improving my relationship with Jack. I started meeting with him three to four times a week in the morning to talk about anything that we thought each other should know about, or to come up with solutions to any of our operational problems.

At first I could see that Jack didn't seem to really want to stop to talk and he didn't really have much to discuss. I would bring up topics and then ask for his input. I listened to Jack's responses and would have him implement the changes he suggested. Then, Jack requested that we discuss some items. This was a first for him to initiate our agenda. He was very open to giving his input on the different topics I had mentioned. Our relationship had measurably grown, and I could see that Jack was interacting with the operational people far more openly.

I learned that I lead best when I lead by example and that becoming an active listener is hard work, but it helps build strong relationships. Check out the area where you would like to see your team members grow and improve, and then model that behavior and take the time to really listen. You'll benefit by empowering your team and strengthening your personal and business relationships."

Focus Groups

You know how it feels when someone truly listens to you and makes you feel as if your opinion counts. Once, a market research group called to ask me about my traveling, flying patterns and habits. After asking me several questions on the telephone, the interviewer invited me to participate in a focus group. I checked my schedule and found that I could be there. The interviewer agreed to provide me with dinner and pay me $50. Having never participated in a focus group, I thought it would be interesting. A day later, I received a letter of confirmation. The following day, I got another phone call, and finally, the day of the meeting, just before I was supposed to be there, we received yet another reminder call confirming my coming!

It was an amazing experience for me! The airline that hired the research group cared enough about positioning its message and providing service that it took the time to interview hundreds of people and pay thousands of dollars in direct and indirect costs to determine how to price and position its service.

The lesson I learned from this experience is the importance of asking for and listening to the feedback I receive from my prospects and customers. The interviewer who questioned me was very skillful at probing, exploring, clarifying and asking questions over and over in several different ways. The benefit you will gain from this is a more directed message. You will position yourself to communicate for results.

Mom

Koll, the comptroller of a Seattle construction company, told our Leadership Development LAB how he'd helped his mother sell her home and buy another one. She told Koll, "You're so different from your brother. He's always pushing me, telling me what to do and trying to get me to do what he wants me to do." What great secret did Koll use to help his mother break out of her pattern? What powerful, persuasive, motivational tool did he use? Instead of nagging and pushing and telling his mother, he listened, listened and listened.

Why do we sometimes nag instead of listen, combat one another instead of communicate? Here are some suggestions for the listening leader:

1.   **Remain Neutral.** Do not give advice, agree, disagree, criticize, or interrupt. Put judgments on hold.

2.   **Give Your Complete Attention**. Let the other person know you are listening. Maintain constant eye contact, nod your head. Sometimes it is useful to clear your desk or put down your papers. Do not yawn.

3.   **Ask About the Person's Statements.** Dig out *information*. Invite the other person to tell as much as possible. Ask, "Is there anything else?"

4.   **Re-state Main Points.** This assures your listeners you understand their concerns.

5.   **Reach Agreement.** Summarize what you both have said. Encourage the speaker to suggest the next step or course of action.

Listening skills can be tough to master. Maximum listening skills, hearing beyond words and understanding the feelings that exist beneath these words, protects and nourishes successful relationships. You can learn to become an excellent listener with practice and patience. We speak at a rate of about 280 words per minute. We think at a rate of about 1,600 words per minute. Translation: It's very difficult for us to keep our attention on a speaker, since we're thinking at a far greater rate of speed.

An associate at Turbo Management Systems and I visited with a prospective client on a Monday, after having spent the entire day with the organization just the Friday before. We went back for only one purpose: to ensure we really understood their wants and needs. We outlined our understanding with a few suggestions, asked questions and listened for a response. As it turned out, we had misunderstood a few points originally. We walked out with more confidence, more enthusiasm, and a new client. Our listening skills helped make a sale. Take time to really listen and ask questions for clarification.

Listen With Empathy

The next time someone on your team tells you about a problem, don't be so quick to find a solution. Instead, pause, and let people know they've been heard. I promise, pausing will help build your relationships. Your empathy will create a marriage of the minds.

Empathy is the ability to appreciate the other person's feelings without becoming so emotionally involved that your judgment is affected. Empathy is accepting a person without approving or disapproving of what that person says or does. If you listen with empathy, people freely express themselves without fear of being condemned, chastised or ridiculed. You need not agree with another person's values, but you show your respect for the person's feelings.

We often confuse sympathy with empathy, but there's an important difference. Sympathy carries judgment. When you sympathize, you feel sorry for someone, which automatically puts you in a higher, or more advantageous position. When you empathize, you and the other person remain at the same level. Empathetic communication allows you to acknowledge feelings without losing your neutrality. Here are a few examples of empathy vs. sympathy:

Empathy: "I have a sense this is really frustrating for you. I feel we can work together on a solution."

Sympathy: "You're really upset, you poor thing. I'm sorry."

Empathy: "I can see that you're really angry. I need to be able to talk to you, but I can't when you're swearing and calling people names. I really want to hear what you have to say."

Sympathy: "I'm upset you're so angry with me. I feel bad for you that you don't know how to control your temper."

Empathy is also about connection. A person doesn't have to be in trouble or upset for you to listen with empathy. The person who listens for emotional cues and responds to them has the mark of leadership.

In an empathy statement, you identify how you think the other person feels and why. For example, "It sounds like you feel you were left out of that discussion when I didn't ask for your opinion." In this example, the feeling was being left out and the reason was because I did not ask for your opinion. This empathy statement should make the person feel that you understand them better, thus improving communication.

As a team leader you can use empathy statements:

* To help reduce strong emotions that can stand in the way of rational thinking. Making an empathy statement to someone expressing anger can often diffuse some feelings about an issue. For example, "I can see that you are furious about being embarrassed in front of the team."

* To encourage other people to listen to you. If they feel you are genuinely recognizing their emotions, they are more likely to listen to what you say.

* To relieve some of the anxiety being felt about publicly discussing a problem. For example, "I can understand why it would be very awkward for you to have to reprimand Joe when only a month ago you were working side by side as peers and now you're the boss!"

Note that in both of the above examples, the empathy statement did not include the word "but," which tends to escalate the emotion instead of reducing it, so that the benefit of the empathy statement is lost. An alternative is to explore thoroughly the other person's feelings and position on the subject before presenting your opinion. Use phrases such as, "Another way to look at that is..." or "At the same time my view is..."

Listen To Lead

Glenn, a dentist, told our Leadership Development LAB he'd overheard a conversation between a hygienist and an assistant. The hygienist, Kristy, was criticizing Glenn. The gist of the heated discussion was, "He doesn't come over to help me out so I can leave on time and I'm not going to help him anymore. If he won't help me, then I won't help him, either." She said the words with a great deal of venom.

"At first, I felt vindictive. Glen mentioned, 'I won't ask her to do anything for me,' he thought. "I'll show her, I don't need her anyway."

After wasting half a day in emotional upset, Glen settled on a course of action. He concluded that if he were to lead his hygienist into effective performance, he needed to move past petty emotions and really listen for the message behind the upset. He made a list of all her complaints.

"When I looked at them objectively, I realized she was right in a large part of what she said and was justified in her feelings. So I made a decision to pay more attention to her needs. I started to listen and began to look for anything I could do to help her even in the smallest of ways. I asked others of our clinical team to give her all the help they could give, preferably without being asked. I genuinely listened to Kristy, and I asked others to do the same.

Kristy's attitude changed. She since has volunteered to help others in areas that are not her responsibility. One day, she jumped in and helped with an implant impression without being asked. This made the operation easier and faster for me, and more pleasurable for the patient."

Glen learned that you can't lead people without listening to them. "When I became genuinely concerned for Kristy, she expressed genuine concern and interest in and for others," he said.

If a team member is causing you grief, why not turn the tables? Instead of bullying that person into obedience, you can make your mark as a strong leader by listening to the complaints that person has about you. If you are courageous enough, ask people to explain what about you is letting them down. Demonstrate your willingness to change by listening and asking for suggestions. Pay attention to them and their needs. When they respond, you will have re-established rapport, and their behavior will change as well. When they perform work that is approximately right, tell them, "Thanks for the effort!" You will bring out the best and move in a positive way toward building a championship team, one that flies *in formation*.

Active vs. Passive Listening

Confusion in communication often occurs as a result of passive listening. When a message is delivered by the speaker, the listener mentally translates the spoken word into a particular message. This may or may not be the message intended by the speaker. The passive listener accepts their own translation to be accurate. The active listener reflects back to the speaker for more *information* or clarification.

The chance for confusion in a meeting is magnified because there are many "listeners" for every idea, and, therefore, many potential translations. It is critical that the team leader use these active listening skills frequently during the meeting:

When you listen to effect change, that is, listen to lead, consider the following:

1. **Develop powers of concentration.** Learn to ignore distractions. Good listeners will themselves into listening. Actively reduce controllable noise by closing doors, holding calls and clearing your mind of clutter. The more you concentrate while listening, the easier listening becomes.

2. **Overlook mannerisms.** Don't prejudice the value of a message due to a team member's delivery or appearance. Important *information* can be obtained from an unimpressive messenger. The content of a message means more than the way it is packaged.

3. **Focus on key concepts.** Identify the major points of a message. It is difficult to grasp detailed *information* without breaking down the message into key areas. Be sure and re-phrase and repeat those concepts to the speaker to ensure you've got the message correctly.

4. **Hold your fire.** Separate the tasks of interpreting and evaluating. Understand the message before judging it, and resist

the temptation to mentally debate instead of listening. Slow down the listening process by asking questions to check your understanding. Holding your fire also means paying attention to the speaker without mentally framing a response.

5. **Work at listening.** Listening is even more work than talking. This is not the time to relax. If you're actively listening, your body temperature will rise slightly, your heartbeat will increase and your body will pump out higher levels of adrenaline.

6. **Listen to lead.** Take what you've heard to heart and act on important messages and *information*. When your team members realize they've been heard, that you genuinely care and respond to their concerns, they'll willingly fall *in formation* with you.

Ralph Waldo Emerson would often greet his friends by asking, "What's become clearer to you since we last met?" That question is so much more powerful than "What's new?" or "How are you doing?," questions to which people give automatic responses, because they know the person who asked really won't listen for an answer. Emerson's question inspires the respondent to reflect, and also lets the respondent know the person who asked the question will definitely listen for an answer. Further, Emerson didn't tell people his own thoughts until he found out what issues others might have on their minds.

Rephrasing, or reflective listening, is a way of verifying what you think the other person has said. It is much like holding up a mirror and saying, "This is what I understood you to say. Is that right?" The other person will confirm your understanding and will then feel that you understand. Then, if necessary, the speaker will provide clarifying *information*. Rephrasing can be very useful for clarification of people's ideas during discussions and decision making.

As a team leader you can use rephrasing: to clarify your own statements or questions if people do not seem to understand; and to clarify a team member's statements.

Rephrasing statements begin with such phrases as:
What I'm hearing is...
So in other words...
So it sounds like...
Let me make sure I've got this right...

When you put yourself in another person's shoes, your own assumptions and feelings in the background, you open your mind to new ideas. You genuinely seek out the contribution and help fulfill the needs of others. This brings about greater understanding and ultimately enhances morale. Would you like to work for a person you feel understands your needs, or one who is blind to them? Which leader will secure your loyalty? For which leader would you willingly go the extra mile? Leadership isn't so much through the spoken word as the leader's response to the words that are spoken.

Listen to your team. Permit all members to express their ideas. Your aim is to understand their point of view. Paraphrase their points to be sure you understand them to their satisfaction. This sounds easy, but it is not. You will catch yourself making judgments, tuning out, evoking your own thoughts and otherwise failing to really comprehend what the speaker is saying.

The importance of listening cannot be overemphasized. Skill in good listening has a profound effect on the team's productivity. You must listen to each person and prove that you understand. You must establish your intent: "My job is to understand what you have in mind and help your thought along. I am not here to make a judgment." This posture satisfies team members and also creates an atmosphere in which all ideas are considered worthy of team consideration.

Involve every member of the team. Most teams have talkative members and quiet members, and you cannot afford to miss the contributions that the quiet ones can make. Once you have identified the quiet members, be careful not to pin them down; but when you ask for a response, you might rest your eyes on them first, going on to the others only when they give no response. Authentic listening elicits a deeper understanding of the speaker, and the speaker has a discovery of new understanding through the process.

* **Listening shows you care.**
* **Listen to solve problems.**
* **Listen with empathy.**
* **Listen actively.**
* **Listen to lead.**

15 Leadership Principles

1.   Lead from High Ideals.
2.   Become Genuinely Interested.
3.   Don't Criticize, Condemn or Complain.
4.   Acknowledge.
5.   See their Point Of View.
6.   Be an Active Listener.
7.   Play Yourself Down.
8.   Validate their Ideas.
9.   Dramatize your Ideas.
10. Stimulate Competition.
11. When you Blow It, Show It.
12. Avoid Dogmatic Declarations.
13. Avoid Arguments.
14. Begin with Yes, Yes, Yes.
15. Appeal to their Noble Motives.

From Turbo Management Systems
- Leadership Development LAB

>>>18

Loyal Leadership

The true leader is always led.

Carl Jung

Jump In

Jeff, the president and owner of an alloy steel fabricating company, told our Leadership Development LAB about the time he and a friend took a guided rafting trip along the Rogue River in Southern Oregon. One morning, they heard commotion coming from the boat in front of them. People were excitedly shouting about something called the 'Sports Illustrated Rock.' Ron, a middle-aged man, and his two sons, began frantically rowing to the side of a 50- to 60- foot rock. To the amazement of the group, he scrambled out of the boat, climbed to the top of the rock, and launched himself into the river. Ron's two sons followed their father to the top of the rock and with a gleeful yell, jumped in one after the other.

Jeff followed Dexter as he crept cautiously to the rock's edge. They stared at what appeared to be about two miles straight down.

"Are you going to jump?" Dexter asked Jeff.

"I don't think so."

"Good!" he replied. "I don't want to jump either."

Both men retreated two steps back.

Jeff said, "I began thinking to myself, I should be able to make this jump. It is obviously safe, the others survived. I realized it was only fear that stood in my way, so I turned around, walked back up to the top of the rock, and without any hesitation took the Big Jump.

When I surfaced, I turned around and looked back up to where Dexter was again peering over the ledge, all alone with his fears. But after some soul searching he too made the jump, and together we swam to shore, got into our raft and resumed our trip down the river.

Dexter and I discussed our jump later in the day as we drifted along in this very special place. We were both exhilarated by being able to overcome our fears and expanding our comfort zone. I could have easily been the last one off the rock if Dexter's fears hadn't stopped him. Or we both could have reinforced each other's fear, letting the fear win, and then neither of us jumping. But we didn't. We conquered the fear."

The brave one who steps forward, faces the fear and makes the leap has stretched farther than the distance of the jump. Where are you holding back? What leap do you need to make? Old paradigms are broken by those who take a leap of faith. Henry Ford took a leap of faith when he bet on the idea that cars could be built for the masses, and the masses would buy them. Bill Gates took a leap of faith when he started Microsoft. Sam Walton took a leap of faith when he started Walmart. There is never enough data to fully support any major move. It takes a leap of faith. This is the day for you to dive in to the challenge of the empowering leader, and many others will follow!

Going The Distance

Red, the superintendent of a highway construction company, told our Leadership Development LAB about his experience in the Hood-to-Coast run, a grueling, two-day road race in Oregon, in which relay teams make their way from the mountains to the beach. Halfway through the race, Red's team was so far behind, it seemed pointless to even continue. (Everyone else would have stretched out and gone home before his group even crossed the finish line.) Red's fellow team members wanted to quit. Then it was Red's turn to run.

He said, "Let's give it one more try."

Red re-doubled his efforts and took five minutes off his time during his 5-mile stint. Then the next team member began, taking five minutes off his five-mile stint. The team began to feel the spark of encouragement. The next runner took five minutes off his time, and the next, another five minutes. The team completed the race successfully! When Red held up his medal for completing the race on time, he was beaming with pride, the pride that comes from re-doubling your commitment to succeed.

One person, one leader, who puts forth that second effort, can actually re-double the commitment of the entire team, causing each individual on the team to perform at a higher level. The entire team exceeds beyond its highest level of expectation. Like geese, when you're pulling together for a greater good, you'll reach that 71 percent advantage.

Try picking a project in which your team has fallen behind. Re-double your individual efforts. You'll be amazed at how others begin to draft off your success. They too begin to apply themselves more fervently and fall into alignment.

Many of us question our skills as leaders. When Red ran his leg of the race, he didn't know in advance that he would take five minutes off his previous time. He didn't know that he would inspire others to improve their performance. Yet, he was a leader in the making. Leadership can be crisply defined as skill in getting people to want to do what needs doing. We all possess a capacity to lead and influence the outcome of events. The only question is to what degree we lead. Leadership is a skill that can be learned. Some people have greater natural aptitudes than others, but that's also true of playing golf, or getting a lawnmower started.

Empowering leaders learn to do five things well:

1. They challenge the process and the status quo. Their motto is: "Let's find a better way."
2. They inspire a shared vision, capturing ideas of the future and communicating it to others.
3. They empower others to act, provide parameters and freedom, do not question judgment, and support the achievements of agreed-upon goals.
4. They model decisiveness, creativity, courage and vulnerability.
5. They encourage and reinforce accomplishment. The empowering leader is in the wings saying, "You can do it!" When accomplishments are achieved, the empowering leader is the first to draw attention to these accomplishments.

Start living an examined life. Be fully aware of what you think and do, and ensure your actions measure up to high standards. The empowering leader is compassionate and able to motivate the team to achieve seemingly impossible tasks. The empowering leader has learned well the lessons of the past, holds strongly to values that preserve the present, and plans for the future, with integrity and dignity. The empowering leader is an inspiration to all and uses skills to cultivate and nurture the physical and intellectual growth of each individual. As a result, the loyalty and admiration returned to the leader transcends the whole team beyond all base or common ideals.

If You Blow It, Show It

Kevin, the training director of an international bakery, told our Leadership Development LAB about how acknowledging his own foibles inspired loyalty from his team:

"I was conducting a training session titled "Commitment to Quality" with 25 of our production employees. One of the first things on the agenda was identifying the barriers to quality in processes, products and performance in our bakery organization. The discussion seemed to quickly digress into a 'management bashing' session," he said.

Kevin said there were numerous comments about, "If management would just ...," or "If management would stop ...," "If it weren't for management ...." He said he could feel the blood climbing up to his neck and his temperature was rising.

"Instead of following my knee-jerk inclination (I really wanted to defend management's position and all of the decisions that I had been a part of), I said, 'You may be right. I, along with the rest of the management team, may have screwed up.'"

Kevin proceeded to recount to the group a specific incident from his own experience of really blowing it. He told our Leadership Development LAB, "I didn't hold anything back. I let it all hang out. I left no room for imagining how big a mistake I had made and could make. I concluded by saying to the production team, 'Managers are just like all the rest of you. We are prone at times to making the same poor decisions and big mistakes you all make. I guess the important thing is that we all learn from our mistakes.'"

The attitudes of our discussion group switched, almost like flipping on a light switch. Everyone began immediately to start productively and objectively brainstorm all kinds of barriers to quality, and they even identified some barriers that included themselves. After we had listed all the 'barriers to quality' they could think of, we had several flip chart pages hung on the walls all around the room. We began to brainstorm possible solutions, ways to overcome these barriers to quality. Numerous solutions were generated and those too were hung on the wall. The positive energy and excitement was intense.

By admitting my errors, faults and foibles, I saw that others could better relate to me, respond and accept me. They no longer felt they have to prove something to me. Others can more easily admit their faults and foibles, and they can also accept the same type of history in themselves. We are all human! It is only then that we can more objectively brainstorm. Stop being judgmental and open up to all possible courses of action and solutions.

The action I call you to is admit to being human! Begin by getting in step with others by pointing out your own faults. We all mess up. You will gain the trust, respect and cooperation of those around you! You will find the blocks to quality, and more important, you will find the answers you need to overcome the barriers to continuous improvement. You will gain the full commitment needed to build a team that solves your quality problems. You will eliminate scrap, shorten cycle time and respond to your customers more quickly. You will cut costs. You will gain the full commitment needed to build a team that soars."

Empowering Leaders Manage Emotions

Cameron, the general manager of a chain of popular restaurants, told our Leadership Development LAB about driving to work one morning. A few minutes away from the restaurant, his Ford Explorer got stuck behind a Cadillac that was creeping along well below the speed limit. Cameron, who is highly energetic, was slowly losing patience with Mr. Cadillac, and began tailing him far too closely. At one point, the Caddie came to a dead stop right in the middle of the intersection, when it had the right-of-way.

"What is this guy doing?" Cameron thought to himself. "You don't have to slow here, you just go!" This forced him to stop right behind the Caddie, at which point he waved his arms in dismay and mouthed words through the windshield to the effect, "What the heck are you doing? Just go!" Cameron recalls. "I could see that Mr. Cadillac noticed my tirade in his rear-view mirror, but he seemed unruffled as he crept through the intersection. Just as he turned, I got a good look at him. Wouldn't you know it? I had been venting my anger at the senior vice president of my company. I could feel my temperature rising as I turned several shades of crimson.

Quickly slumping down into my seat, I sheepishly followed him — at a distance — the rest of the way to work. I parked a good distance from the building and waited for him to enter before I even got out of my car. Gentleman that he is, he never brought up that embarrassing incident."

Cameron learned a powerful lesson about exercising patience, giving the other person the benefit of the doubt. As Cameron put it, "I can be a hustle kind of guy without running over others." On your fast track to success, don't compromise your goals by imposing your pace on others. Slow down. Sometimes, we're in such a hurry to get where we're going, we forget the reason for our journey. Cameron's temper might have cost him his career, all for a few minutes saved in travel time.

At the first session of one of our Leadership LABs in Seattle, one class member arrived with his hand in a cast. Of course, I knew there was a story. He'd listed his home with a real estate agent. Thinking his house had sold, he called the agent, only to discover the agent had not followed through on promises and commitments, and that the sale had failed. The homeowner was so angry that he slammed his fist into the wall and broke his hand. At the same meeting, another class member arrived with a cast on his foot. He had kicked the wall in anger and broke his foot.

Expressing upset is normal. You need to release emotions to live a balanced, successful, empowered life. In fact, when you bottle up negative feelings, they tend to explode. Yet there's a difference between expressing your anger in a healthy manner and blowing your top. Strong leaders don't lose their temper. Imagine a piece of tempered steel; it's hard and keeps its edge. It has great strength. When steel loses its temper, a result of over-heating, the steel is no longer sharp. The same thing happens to us when we overheat. We no longer have full value and strength. We lose our edge when we lose our tempers. We lose our personal and competitive edge. We lose the edge of a winning team committed to results.

In one class a manager, talking about the bad-tempered president of his organization, asked, "How does he expect us to look up to him and respect him as a professional if he can't keep from losing his temper just because the conference door is locked?"

I asked, "What are you talking about?"

He said, "We had a meeting scheduled in the conference room, and when we got there, the door was locked. He started cursing, 'No wonder this business can't make a profit; they can't even get the #!!** door unlocked when we want it.' Perhaps this president felt he was demonstrating great strength as a tough leader. Yet the opposite occurred. He lost ground with key team members and with anyone else who overheard his little temper tantrum. People who cannot control themselves cannot lead effectively. They inspire little loyalty and set a poor example for others to follow. As it turned out, this president was fired a few months later by the board of directors.

Unlike the proverbial loose cannon, some people have a low-grade, just-below-the-surface anger, which colors all they do, feel and say. It colors how they relate to others. This low-grade anger stems from resentments and frustrations tied to unresolved issues with family, friends, bosses or former bosses. They collect little grudges, and before they know it, they're laden with a big bag of grudges. Dragging around a bag of grudges takes tremendous energy. You're so worn out from the burden, there's no energy left for work, fun and the vital living necessary for a dynamic leader.

If you've been carrying around a grudge bag, cut out the bottom and let the grudges fall away. Make a list of all the people you believe have hurt you and next to their name, write that you forgive them. "I forgive Charlie for not giving me the raise I deserved." And most importantly, forgive yourself. Repeat the process until you feel as if you have genuinely forgiven all those you believe have wronged you. This is a painful process, as you bring to the surface all your old wounds. Yet, once that anger floats away, you will rise to a higher level, the level of true leadership.

Are you slamming your fist into the wall? Are you allowing anger to drain your vitality? Act now. Release the resentments you've been nursing. Reclaim your energy and vitality. You will amaze yourself with your new level of personal power and achievement.

Empowered leaders also understand a fundamental truth about emotion. They do not judge others. They try to walk in another person's shoes.

Roger, the operation team leader for a wholesale electrical distributor, told our Leadership Development LAB about his stint as a children's shoe salesman, which ended in 1970.

"After years of putting up with smelly feet," Roger began, "I decided to change vocations. I submitted my two week's notice and impatiently waited for my last day to arrive. I decided early on the morning of my final day to unload on the first customer who dared irritate me. After all, what could the customer do? Tell the boss?"

As it turned out, everyone was nice to Roger that day. The kindness did nothing to deter his plans. Then, just before closing a woman came into the store with three small children in tow. Most kids just destroyed the children's area, but these three wreaked havoc on every inch of the store. They used their arms to sweep shoes off all the racks. They yelled and screamed. Their mother made no effort to correct their wild behavior.

This was just the customer Roger had been waiting for. "As I sat before her on the fitting stool, trying to lace a shoe on one of her monster's kicking feet while another joyfully punched me from behind, I knew the time was right to strike. 'Lady,' I said, 'I've seen a lot of misbehaving kids, but without a doubt, these are the most out-of-control, horrible monsters I have ever seen. Anyone who would allow children to behave like this doesn't deserve to call herself a parent.'

Roger waited for a counter-attack, having saved his best lines for retaliation. Instead, the woman's eyes filled and in a moment, she burst into tears. "I'm sorry, I'm so ashamed. You're right, since my husband was killed in Vietnam last month, I haven't been able to deal with much of anything," she said. "Please understand, I'm not really a bad mother, at least, I didn't used to be, but I just don't know anymore. I can't cope with my children the way I should."

Needless to say, Roger felt smaller than a pair of baby's booties. He learned a lesson that day that has helped take him high up the corporate ladder: You are not a judge. Don't let your own emotions allow you to attribute meaning to behavior; every situation is unique. Give others the benefit of the doubt. You may never know the other person's story, but behave as if you did. Always try and walk in the other person's shoes.

Empowering Leaders Serve

Great leaders possess a "way of seeing" that inspires giving and sharing actions. They have a deep sense of purpose. They have a set of values that disciplines their behavior to serve others through growth and development. This way of seeing creates an environment of abundance and interdependence (as opposed to scarcity and dependence). They operate to remove barriers and provide pathways and road maps to encourage creative involvement and participation. In so doing, they operate without limitations. When you place yourself in genuine service of others, you find that others willingly serve your organization, and they inspire others to greatness. Empowering leaders who believe they can learn from every person in the organization encourages learning throughout the team. The learning leader makes team members feel valued, as if their contribution counts. They experience being a part of something bigger than themselves and have a sense of purpose and meaning that goes beyond the pride and satisfaction of simply doing good work.

We once visited with the second-in-command of the Northwest office of an international construction firm. We endeavored to profile the company to gain a clear picture of what was and wasn't working inside the firm, where the opportunities for "wins" were, and where immediate profit-enhancing improvements could be made. We began to ask some of the questions we normally ask: "Tell us a little about the experience, background, tenure of your management team." We learned that most of the top management team (a staff of about twelve) had been with the firm for less than 19 months. There was an extraordinary amount of turnover in the upper and middle ranks of management and had been for some time. Obviously, there had to be a reason for this turnover.

We learned that the general manager (who was the son of the chairman of the board and brother of the president of the firm) had a big ego and was prone to losing his temper and throwing little tantrums. The manager we met with had been putting up with the inexcusable behavior of this spoiled manager for several years.

The general manager never listened to others. He believed only he had the answers; he believed he knew everything. He had nothing to learn. As it happened, one of this company's former project managers was participating in our Leadership Development LAB. He told us that he tendered his resignation the day after meeting with this general manager when he took over the Seattle office! He wasn't the only one who was totally turned off by this egocentric behavior. This firm got exactly what it deserved. All the real professionals were leaving. They felt put off by the general manager's ego, and felt he was blind to all their thoughts and ideas.

This is not the first time we have heard these stories about leaders who refuse to learn. Of course, when you're the owner (or, in this case, the son of the owner), you can get away with almost anything. This branch office was losing money. The president, who was located in another country, blamed the other local managers and other staff members, the economy, and unfair competition — not his brother, the general manager. Would the president open his mind and listen? I don't know. It is a fact that incompetent management can survive only when others support it. This is called "enabling behavior." Enabling behavior tolerates, puts up with, and excuses unskilled, inexcusable behavior. This firm's management had been exercising enabling behavior with this general manager for quite a while.

One of the skills of an empowered leader is intervention. Empowered leaders recognize when a mistake has been made — even when it's their own — and willingly try other methods. They willingly learn from their errors. These leaders help team members see how disruptive their behavior is and what skills they need to develop to positively impact and empower (versus disrupt and disempower) the entire team. Intervention holds up a mirror for others to see themselves clearly.

By learning from your associates and learning from your mistakes, you build a winning team of strong champions. You attract winners and keep winners. You break through to new heights of achievement. Learning from your errors means that you have to shed any facade about your power and authority. You need to let the real you shine through, warts and all.

"And A Little Child Shall Lead Them"

Glen, a Portland area dentist, told our Leadership Development LAB about an experience that served as a metaphor for the importance of revealing one's self. A new federal regulation required him to wear, for safety reasons, a mask and goggle-like protective eye wear.

"My patients referred to me as the Lone Ranger, the masked bandit, Batman, Monkey Man and Space Man," Glen said. Wearing this protective garb had become as routine as putting on his socks or combing his hair. It has become so routine that he took wearing it for granted -- that is, when he had it on he was not aware of it and when he had the gear off he felt as though he had it on.

"It was not unusual for someone at the supermarket to ask, 'What's that blue thing around your neck?' And accidentally leaving the mask on sure is an effective way, when driving on the freeway going home from work, to get people to smile when they see me. I sometimes wonder why they're smiling until I get home and my son Zach says, 'Hey, Dad, you still have your mask on.'

"One day, I was treating a rather bright and very precocious 10-year old girl. When I came into the treatment room and faced her, she cocked her head to one side, raised one eyebrow, wrinkled her forehead and then asked, 'Who are you?' in a rather insistent tone. The tone of her voice and look on her face I'll never forget; I felt very foolish.

"What I learned from these experiences is that people want the health protection we give them, and yet they also need to know who is treating them. So I now remove my mask and goggles and get eye to eye contact at least once in each appointment. I build better relationships when I remove my mask and deal person-to-person with my patients."

Explore the masks you have been wearing as a leader. Take them off and deal with people with all guards removed. For some of you this could mean taking off your necktie or coming around and sitting on the other side of the desk. Take a look. Are you hiding behind your title, your age, your education, or your experience? If so, drop your guard and let people really know and see you. It's the only way people feel valuable. You will acquire meaningful relationships that empower and build a bonded championship team.

It's An Old Story

Imagine you're walking across the hot desert with the sun beating down on your head. You are hot and tired. Worst of all, you're thirstier than you've ever been. You come over a little knoll and find a water pump on the other side. It's a rusty old pump set on a rickety platform. On its handle hangs a tin cup, and tied fast to the tin cup is a note. The note reads:

"This pump will draw water if you go at it right. Under the rock, you will find a bottle of water. If you pour the water into the top of the pump, and then pump like crazy, I promise you will get all the water you can drink -- good, clear, sweet and cold. I know the pump works. I fixed it last week. I also know you'll want to immediately just drink from the bottle, but I'm warning you, if you drink any from the bottle, that's all the water you'll get. It takes the entire bottle to prime the pump. Good luck.

P.S. When you've had your fill of water, fill the bottle and put it under the rock for the next fellow."

It takes great faith to pour the water down the staff of the rusty old pump instead of down your raspy, dry throat. It takes generosity to refill the bottle with water before proceeding on your weary way.

What, you may ask, does a bottle of water in the desert have to do with empowering leadership? Great leaders possess great faith. We have all experienced plenty of let-down and failure. Still, the empowering leader doesn't give up on the human race. Empowering leaders set aside cynicism and trust that the team will not let them down. They recognize that one generous turn deserves another. Every person I have met in a position of significant authority and power made his or her way to the top by respecting and trusting others. Leaders do not reach leadership all on their own. Others support them in their journey, or they serve as models for the leader to follow. In the words of Isaac Newton, "If I can see farther, it is because I have stood on the shoulders of giants."

We stand on the shoulders of those who came before us, who left something behind that we can leverage, if we possess faith and trust. It is a measure of our own character how much we leave behind for those who follow. Today would be a great day for you to check. Ask yourself, what am I leaving behind? What is my legacy for those who follow?

People don't want to be managed. They want to be led. There is no such thing as a world manager, but there are great world leaders.

There lives inside each of us a genius, a capacity, an untapped potential. This possibility for being and becoming is seen in the shadows of our past achievements, the mist of dreams and aspirations. We tap our potential for leadership by gaining confidence from those who came before us, by accepting responsibility for our present mission, and by committing to our vision for the future.

Summary Steps to Get and Stay *In Formation*

* Include Everyone in the Mission and Vision.

*Agree to Values for the Voyage.

* Embrace Change as your Constant Companion.

*Team Accepts Accountability for its Performance.

* Let your Customers be your Compass.

* Know your Processes.

* Keep Meaningful Measurements.

* Set Stretching Goals.

* Train to Ensure Gains.

* Make Stretching Commitments.

* Encouragement Is Your Way Of Being.

* Coach for Coninuous Improvement.

* Mistakes Are Your Classroom.

* Solve Problems Permanently.

* Maximize Meetings.

* Listen, Really Listen.

* Everyone Is the Leader.

Larry W. Dennis, Sr. President
Turbo Management Systems

About The Author

Larry W. Dennis is the energetic founder of Turbo Management Systems™. The author of the successful book, *Repeat Business*, and his new book, *Making Moments Matter*, shares the philosophy behind his ability to improve profits for hundreds of businesses whose key managers have learned the important principles of empowering leadership and superior customer service. Dennis is the inventor of the patented video training system, Psycho-Actualized Learning, and is a dedicated father and grandfather who has been profiled in "Secrets of Raising Teenagers Successfully." Dennis also served on the Business Advisory Council of Warner Pacific College.

For more information about Turbo Management Systems™, Leadership Team Advance, Leadership Development Lab, or Performance Team training, visit www.turbomgmt.com or contact:

Turbo Management Systems
(503) 625-1867 / Fax: (503) 625-2699
larry@turbomgmt.com

MAKING MOMENTS MATTER provides powerful time management tools to help you become more organized and productive in your professional and personal lives. 89 time management tools provide insight into how to make the most of every precious minute of every day.

"Often I find myself frantically busy all day long, pecking at one task after another. By the end of the day, I would have nothing substantial accomplished and very little to show for my efforts. *Making Moments Matter* helped me identify and prioritize what is important. Stay on task, and, most importantly, have a sense of accomplishment by the end of the day. As Larry says, it is not about "time management", it's about making the most of your life. Time is the only true absolute. How we use it is what sets us apart in both business and life. *Making Moments Matter* has helped me make better use of my time, absolutely."

Chuck Hayward, Architect
Ankrom Moisan Associated Architects

ISBN 0-9631766-4-4 $16.95

EMPOWERING LEADERSHIP helps you understand the
Fifteen Fundamental Leadership Principles needed to tap your
team's full potential. You see how to bring out the best in yourself
and others. Whether you are a manager, supervisor, team leader
or committee chair, you are shown how to exercise empowering
leadership.

"Page after page the wisdom of your book provides valuable tools
I apply daily to raise our team to higher levels of accomplishment."

Ron Warman, General Manager
Ron's Automotive

ISBN 0-9631766-1-7 $24.95

***HOW TO TURBO CHARGE YOU - 6 Steps to Tap Your
True Potential*** guides you to an understanding of your unique
talents and abilities. You see for the first time how to leverage
your past successes. Written with real life examples, in an enter-
taining style, *How to Turbo Charge You* equips you with the 14
tools needed to thrive in a time of uncertainty and accelerated
change.

"Larry has created an outline for the road to success both personally
and professionally. A must read for all employers and employees.
It's the best self-help book we've read in years - he simplifies
everything and then takes you through the steps."

Lin and John Damrell, Owner/Operator
Budget-Rent-A-Car, five franchises

ISBN 0-9631766-2-5 $14.95

REPEAT BUSINESS teaches your new and long-term employees the six steps to superior customer service, the skills that will help you create loyal customers. Written in straightforward, plain language and colorful anecdotes, *Repeat Business* helps you learn how to treat people so they keep coming back as satisfied customers.

"What a great book! It is a must for all employee manuals in companies of all sizes. You are right, customers are less and less tolerant of companies that don't show a caring attitude."
    Bob Ulrich, Marketing Director, Dial One Northwest, Inc.

ISBN 0-9631766-0-9 $9.95

THE GREAT BASEBALL CAP - This 32-page character building children's story is illustrated with warm 5-color pencil drawings. *The Great Baseball Cap* inspires 4 to 12-year old readers to take pride in their personal appearance, value relationships with their parents, siblings, and friends, and most important of all, value themselves. *The Great Baseball Cap* literally takes the young reader to the point of affirming **"I AM A WINNER!"**

"Your book is a winner. It will help every young reader become a winner and build resolute self-confidence and the ability to feel good about themselves and achieve. That's my endorsement."
Mark Victor Hansen, *Chicken Soup for the Soul* books

ISBN 0-9631766-5-X $9.95

TURBO MANAGEMENT SYSTEMS PROCESSES

Comprehensive Organizational Analysis (COA): Organizational strengths are analyzed for clarity and focus. Customer Opinion and Employee Opinion Surveys measure strengths and weaknesses of your organization. This provides direction for a breakthrough to "World-Class" performance.

Leadership Team Advance (LTA): Top leadership team assesses its strengths and areas for needed improvement. The leadership team aligns its efforts with organizational objectives, and prepares to align each department. Team members develop action plans with built-in follow-up and accountabilities to insure immediate results and improved performance.

Cultural Quality Awareness (CQA): The entire company experiences a "milestone day," establishing continuous improvement as a way of life. Suppliers and customers are invited to clarify what is and is not working in achieving your desired level of excellence. Internal customers are asked for feedback on current levels of performance, and action plans for improved responsiveness are created.

Quality Steering Team (QST): A cross-section of organizational team members is commissioned to lead the continuous implementation and measurement of *your* quality improvement efforts -- in effect, to keep you on course with your improvement journey.

Leadership Development Lab (LDL): All key team members develop essential communication and leadership skills to maximize the effectiveness of the entire organization. Participants develop the insights, skills and abilities to empower everyone in the organization to peak performance.

Performance Team Lab (PTL): Everyone understands the purposes of performance teams and masters the skills and techniques that make teams successful. Teams learn effective problem-solving techniques and self-management methods to improve their processes and effectiveness, allowing for and encouraging continuous improvement.

Continuous Improvement Coaching (CIC): Sustaining Your Commitment to Ongoing Improvement...Planning and coaching in targeted areas where continuous improvement is identified, including customer service, sales, supervision, process improvement and problem-solving.

Turbo Sales System (TSS): This system turbo-charges your sales team's skills, heightens their motivation and increases organizational abilities. TSS dramatically improves sales effectiveness by experientially improving key interpersonal sales skills and developing a proven method of organization and accountability.

Superior Customer Service (SCS): Produces a transformation in which all team members approach their daily activities from the customer's point of view, resulting in greater cooperation and a positive approach to excellence and follow-through.

Managing Customer Relations (MCR): Designed to help your team develop and deliver "World-Class Service." Delivering superior, cost-effective service is the element that differentiates "World-Class" companies from their competitors.

Construction Partnering for Success (CPS): Partnering reframes and moves owners, contractors, engineers, and inspectors from confrontation to alliance -- a pledge of cooperation.

TURBO
MANAGEMENT SYSTEMS

36280 NE Wilsonville Rd.
Newberg, OR 97132
(503) 625-1867 / Fax: (503) 625-2699
www.turbomgmt.com

Order Form

Please send me

___ copies of *In Formation* @ $19.95 each
___ copies of *Empowering Leadership* @ $24.95
___ copies of *Repeat Business* @ $9.95
___ copies of *How To Turbo-Charge You* @ $14.95
___ copies of *Communicating For Results* @ $ 9.95
___ copies of *Making Moments Matter* @ $9.95
___ copies of *The Great Baseball Cap* (a children's story)
     @ $9.95

❏ Please send me at no charge complete information about the training services of Turbo Management Systems.™

Add $2.00 for shipping and handling for first item and $1.00 for each additional item, for a total amount of $_____.

❏ Check enclosed   ❏ Bill my MasterCard/VISA

Account #_____

Expires_____ Signature_____

Ship to (Please allow 4 - 6 weeks for delivery):
Name:_____
Address:_____

_____
City/State/Zip:_____
Phone:_____

Mail or fax your order to:
Turbo Management Systems ™
36280 N.E. Wilsonville Rd.
Newberg, Oregon 97132
Phone: (503) 625-1867 / Fax: (503) 625-2699
Email: turbo@turbomgmt.com